Weird Florida

BARNES
& NOBLE
BOOKS

NEW YORK

WEiRD FLORiDA

Your Travel Guide to Florida's Local Legends and Best Kept Secrets

Charlie Carlson

WEIRD FLORIDA

2005 Barnes & Noble Books
Barnes & Noble Publishing
122 Fifth Avenue
New York, NY 10011

ISBN 0-7607-5945-6

First Printing

Printed and bound in
the United States of America

Weird Florida is intended as entertainment to present a historical record of local legends, folklore, and sites throughout Florida. Many of these legends and stories cannot be independently confirmed or corroborated, and the author and publisher make no representation as to their factual accuracy. The reader should be advised that many of the sites described in *Weird Florida* are located on private property and such sites should not be visited, or you may face prosecution for trespassing.

DEDICATION

I would like to dedicate this book to those special Floridians who volunteer so much of their time on preservation projects to save our state's heritage, wildlife, and fragile environment. The "real" Florida will survive only through your unselfish efforts.

I would also like to recognize my children, Erika, Joyce, and Charlie III, and my grandsons, Charlie IV and Andrew—thanks for putting up with my bizarre personality, as it will only get worse. To my best friend, Dot—you've always been my secret inspiration behind the scenes. To my two boxers, Bubba James and Miss Scarlett—thanks for spending time in the kennel while I went in search of Florida's weirdness. And finally, a big thanks to all my readers and fans for your many strange contributions over the years. You have been a great resource for me.

—Charlie Carlson

CONTENTS

FOREWORD

by Mark Sceurman and Mark Moran

Our weird journey began a long, long time ago in a far-off land called New Jersey. Once a year or so, we'd compile a homespun newsletter called *Weird N.J.*, then pass it on to our friends. The pamphlet was a collection of odd news clippings, bizarre facts, little-known historical anecdotes, and anomalous encounters from our home state. The newsletter also included the kinds of local legends that were often whispered around a particular town but seldom heard outside the community where they had originated.

We had started *Weird N.J.* with the simple theory that every town in the state had at least one good tale to tell. The publication soon become a full-fledged magazine, and we made the decision to actually do all of our own investigating to see if we could track down where all of these seemingly unbelievable stories were coming from. Was there, we wondered, any factual basis for these fantastical local legends that people were telling us about? Armed with not much more than a camera and a notepad, we set off on a mystical journey of discovery. Much to our amazement, a lot of what we had initially presumed to be nothing more than urban legend turned out to be real—or at least contained a grain of truth, which had sparked the lore to begin with.

After a dozen years of documenting the bizarre, we were asked to write a book about our adventures, and so *Weird N.J.: Your Travel Guide to New Jersey's Local Legends and Best Kept Secrets* was published in 2003. Soon, people from all over the country began writing to us, telling us about strange tales in their home states. As it turned out, what we had perceived to be something of very local interest was actually just a small part of a larger and more universal phenomenon. People had strange tales to tell that they believed to be true, and all they wanted was somebody to tell them to.

When Barnes & Noble, the publisher of the book, asked us what we wanted to do next, the answer was simple. "We'd like to do a book called *Weird U.S.*, in which we could document the local legends and strangest stories from all over the country," we told them. So for the next twelve months, we set out in search of weirdness wherever it might be found in the fifty states. And indeed, we found plenty of it!

After *Weird U.S.* was published, we came to the conclusion that this country had more great tales than could be contained in just one book. Everywhere we looked, we found unwritten folklore, creepy cemeteries, cursed locations, and outlandish roadside oddities. With this in mind, we told our publisher that we wanted to document it ALL and to do it in a series of books, each focusing on the peculiarities of a particular state.

When the question arose as to which states to cover first, Florida, with its sheer wealth of weird material, rose to the top of the list. And there was only one man who we felt could capture all of the Sunshine State's weirdness in words—Charlie Carlson.

Charlie has been documenting the weirdness of Florida in his books and other publications for years. We ran into him while doing *Weird U.S.*, to which he generously contributed some tales. His stories—not only of local legends and lore but also of the unusual and the unexpected in the history of Florida—were all told in a voice that could only come from a true native, something that is rather rare in his part of the world. When it came to the odd sites and unexplained goings-on around Florida, Charlie seemed to know it all, from the lost spirits who roam the swampy backwaters of the state to the eccentric roadside curiosities that line the tourist-laden roadways. His incredible body of weird work was surpassed by only one thing: his passionate enthusiasm for the discovery of the really strange. Charlie is a true fellow traveler in our search for the bizarre.

So read on and let him be your tour guide through one of the most intriguing and bewildering states of them all. It's a place we like to call *Weird Florida*.

INTRODUCTION

Welcome to that weird appendage attached to the lower southeastern portion of the United States. This is Florida, America's only peninsula state, a useful geographical feature that helps us quickly locate North America on any map. Florida was the landfall for early explorers arriving in the New World, and today it's the launching pad for explorations into the mysteries of the universe. Here in the Sunshine State, you can stand in the oldest city in the nation, St. Augustine, and watch the space shuttle streak off into some unknown vastness.

There's another weird thing about Florida—it has a strange magnetism that's been attracting humans for untold eons. Ninety percent of Floridians are from some other place, and this is what makes me one of the weird things about this book. Given the fact that I am a tenth-generation Floridian, some folks might consider me a walking human oddity.

The roles that my ancestors had played in Florida's past have inspired my interest in Florida's history and folklore. For example, my ancestor Colonel William Williams was captured by the Spanish in 1810 and thrown into the dungeon of the old Castillo de San Marcos in St. Augustine. Williams was part of a group called the East Florida Patriots, who were fighting for independence from Spain. Anyway, Williams apparently had quite a hand with a fiddle, which helped him pull off the weirdest escape ever made from the old fort. He was called on to play his fiddle at a fiesta for the Spanish governor. The more he fiddled, the more rum the Spaniards drank. When they became sufficiently smashed, Colonel Williams made his escape. That's the sort of crazy stuff that you won't find in mainstream history books. You have to search for it, like the other weird things that are awaiting you in Florida.

In the course of my explorations, I have come to realize that there are really three Floridas. The first is the artificial Florida, the one made of concrete, theme parks, billboards, condominiums, and swarms of tourists. The second is what we natives call the "Real Florida," the one that few tourists seldom venture into. It's the one with swamps, snakes, fish camps, gators, and swarms of mosquitoes. But there is a third Florida, a sometimes elusive one; it's the eccentric one that is woven into the fabric of the other two. Florida is a mixture of fact, fantasy, and folklore, and they are not always easy to separate. That is what gives the state its unique culture.

This book is a detour off the main tourist paths, down a few side roads, through old and new legends, local myths, and whatever else fits the category of weird. But be warned—some of it might be best left alone. Some abandoned places are hazardous; some remote creeks or ponds are dangerous; and gators will eat you. And should you encounter the infamous Florida Skunk Ape, do not attempt to hit him with a big stick. Instead, take a photograph and send it to me.

It would be impossible to pack every weird or mysterious thing about Florida into a single book. What is presented here is a mere sampling of the state's unusual side. Certainly, there's more to be discovered, but for now, let this be your detour around the mundane and onto roads less traveled through the wonderful and weird state of Florida.

—Charlie Carlson

Local Legends

There are plenty of legends in Florida, and
they can be plenty weird. Local legends are
usually passed down orally from one generation to
the next and are seldom found in written records,
until somebody writes a book. What separates a
local legend from general folklore is its restriction to
a specific region. There are general legends that we
have all heard about, but learning about a local one
requires being in contact with local folks.

Legends are good exercise for the imagination. If
our belief is strong enough, we may even become
part of a legend by thinking we see something that
isn't there. . . . Or was it? Was it the wind or that
legendary shape-shifting demon that rippled through
the leaves? After all, we've heard the legend, so it
might be true — or at least some part of it.

Whether ancient or recent, legends are a
significant part of our culture. A sociologist once
wrote, "A culture without traditional mythology is
not a culture."

In the following local legends, you will find a
mixture of ghosts, demons, natural wonders, and,
yes, a significant bit of factual history. The trick is in
screening fact from fiction. But keep this in mind
too: One of these far-fetched tales could be true!

The Devil's Millhopper

Northwest of Gainesville, Florida, is a gigantic, funnel-shaped hole in the ground that is an astonishing five hundred feet across, a hundred and twenty feet deep, and nearly a half mile around its rim. The shape of this geological wonder, now owned by the state, reminded pioneers of a hopper on a gristmill, which held corn as it was fed into the grinder. When prehistoric bones were found in the bottom of the hole, people claimed it was a hopper that fed bodies to the devil, hence the name "Devil's Millhopper," a portal straight to hell.

Weird Florida arrived at this odd cavity early one morning, just in time to break the spiderwebs strung across the path leading to it. The hole can hardly be seen until you are on its rim. The foliage around the edges hides the blackness below, and what look like bushes hiding the opposite side are really the tops of trees that are growing down in the hole. The only way to fully appreci-

ate this dark hole would be to clear all the trees away, and of course, we don't want to do that.

Among the many weird stories about this hole, the earliest derives from Indian legends about a princess whom the devil wanted to marry and who, to make a long legend short, ended up being swallowed by the hole. Another tale, dating from the 1880s, is about a pioneer family that, on its way to town with a wagonload of cotton, saw the hole open up and gobble up an acre of tall pines. According to a preacher who told their story, "The ground began rumbling like Satan himself was coming out of the earth, then a big, frightening hole opened up swallowing trees, rocks, and at least one liquored-up sinner." The Devil's Millhopper was well known for devouring sinners. A traveling evangelist preached, "It's the gateway to hell; the devil's own door!"

More recent yarns claim that a man once fell in and was swallowed up. If that's true, it means the poor soul

ended up in our drinking water, since an aquifer is directly beneath the hole.

A wooden stairway of 236 steps leads from the rim down to a viewers' platform in the Millhopper's bottom. Even on hot days, it remains pleasantly cool in the basin. There are twelve springs in the bottom and a diversity of plant species resembling the flora found in the Appalachian Mountains.

The real story behind this cavity, according to a state geologist, is that it's an ancient sinkhole, formed probably in two stages, the first about ten thousand years ago and the second about a thousand years ago.

The Gateway to Hell?

Have you ever been to the Devil's Millhopper in Gainesville? It is a deep hole that you can go down in. It is about 200 feet deep. Before they built the steps to the bottom, you could walk around the bottom, and in places it was soft like quicksand. I heard that a man got caught in the quicksand one time and disappeared into the ground. They say it is the gateway to hell, but I don't think so. But I really think that you could be sucked into the aquifer in the bottom of that place. I think that's why they put the steps and railings in there—to keep people from getting sucked underground.—*gogator*

An Indian Legend

I'm fourteen years old, and I heard a folklore story about the Devil's Millhopper and how the devil wanted to marry an Indian princess and she refused to marry him, so he came after her. The Indian braves fought him off, but he returned to his doorway to hell, which is the Millhopper. The Indian braves went in after him but he devoured them and spit their bones out to the surface. That's why prehistoric bones are often found in the basin. Of course that's just a story.—*Sarah14*

People Have Vanished There

They say that several people have been to the Devil's Millhopper and have never been seen again. It is supposed to be the biggest sinkhole in Florida.—*student 223*

Just a Big Sinkhole

The Devil's Millhopper is just a big sinkhole. I know a man who collects fossils, and he has a collection of bones that he got from the springs in the bottom of this hole. He has bones from mastodon, giant sloth, huge shark teeth, and other prehistoric fossils that he found in the Devil's Millhopper.—*Jason*

Mastodon teeth

Warning: Florida Can Swallow Us Up in a Moment

The Devil's Millhopper is an example of how dangerous Florida can be; these sinkholes can open up anywhere in the state. I remember when that big one opened up in downtown Winter Park in the 1970s. It swallowed an entire city block, including a car lot with expensive cars. Everything disappeared down the hole into the earth. The Winter Park sinkhole is on Fairbanks Ave. and is a lake today. The Devil's Millhopper should be a warning to all of us how the earth can swallow us up in a moment.—*Randy K.*

Slimy Creatures Live in the Bottom of the Millhopper

The Millhopper is a big sinkhole, and in the bottom of this sinkhole are holes that blind creatures crawl out of. They say these creatures are like big salamanders, but they are blind, because they live in total darkness underground in the aquifer. My question is what does this do to us, because the aquifer is like a big water storage tank for all of the drinking water in Florida. It is a weird thought to think we have slimy creatures swimming around in our drinking water.—*Mace*

Florida's Haunted Oaks

Why is it that half the oak trees in Florida seem to be haunted? Just ask around, and sooner or later, you'll hear a haunted-oak-tree story. There's a ghost oak with an iron chain through it in Fernandina that marks the location of a pirate's treasure. However, this tree is invisible, and you can see it only if you go there with a shovel intending to dig up the buried booty. Of course, how would you know the location of the treasure if you can't see the tree?

There's another oak, in Seminole County, with a man hanging from it. Well, he doesn't hang there all the time, just on certain moonlit nights.

You'll find haunted oaks, usually with some poor soul dangling from a limb, in Brooksville, Winter Garden, Ormond Beach, Tallahassee, and Oviedo. Based on weird stories sent to us by well-informed folks, we decided to hit the road and investigate three of the most popular haunted oaks—that is, if they really existed.

The Devil's Tree

In Port St. Lucie, there's a big oak in a county park on Canal C-24 that has an evil reputation. It is the Devil's Tree, an old oak tree located in Oak Hammock Park, a place frequented mostly by local fishermen who use the boat-launching facilities.

The story begins on January 8, 1971, long before Hammock Park was built, when a serial killer sexually molested and mutilated two teenage girls and then hanged them from the oak tree. The psycho killer then buried his two victims in a shallow grave beneath the oak. Allegedly, the crazed killer returned on several occasions to have his way with the decomposing bodies.

In January 1977, almost on the sixth anniversary of the heinous crime, two men found the girls' skeletons, along with two deteriorating ropes tied in a hangman's noose. Ever since then, there have been reports of hooded satanic worshippers dancing around the tree, and some say that you can still hear the screams of the girls. One allegation has it that before the park was built, there were several attempts to cut down the oak, but it seems that chain saws refused to work when near the tree. When men tried to cut it down with a two-man crosscut saw, all the teeth fell out of the blade. Needless to say, the tree is still standing in a small open area down a nature trail.

Witnesses claim that the women's restroom at Oak Hammock Park is haunted by the dead girls. It is said that strange screams have been heard from the restroom and that doors slam shut. Supposedly, there are cold spots in certain areas of the park. What is really strange is that we found no firsthand accounts of these claims. It was always a case of somebody hearing it from someone else. But that's what keeps legends alive.

There were so many reports of devil worship going on at the Devil's Tree that in 1992, a priest performed an exorcism and placed a cross at the base of the oak. A few years ago, there were several instances when the sheriff's department responded to calls about satanic activities in the park, lending more credibility to these legends.

Chased by Weird Men Wearing Hoods

I have my doubts about any ghost story, but I know that some weird-looking men used to be seen out there a lot wearing hoods and long coats. I have heard hundreds of people say how they would chase you if you got too close.–*Mike H.*

Saw a Warlock Ritual

You want to know about the Devil Tree? We used to camp out there often and used to see people wearing hoods and robes around the tree. I was told that these were warlocks performing a ritual. I don't know how true it is, but we saw them.–*JDXfiles*

Girls Hacked to Death at the Devil's Tree

In Oak Hammock at night you can hear two girls being killed. They were hacked to death and hung up in the tree. People say their screams can be heard all around the Devil's Oak. I went there with my bud to check it out. We found the tree, and when we were walking down the trail, we sensed somebody was following us. We hid behind a tree and looked back down the trail and saw a dark figure of a man. We started walking faster and looked back, and this dark figure was still coming behind us. We got to the parking lot and sat in the car but never saw anything come out of the woods. I think we were being followed for some reason.–*bigfoot88*

Serial Killer Was the Real Devil at the Tree

In Port St. Lucie, FL, there is a little town-owned park where serial killer Gerard John Schaefer hanged, then buried 19-year-old Collette Goodenough and Barbara Ann Wilcox at the Devil's Tree. Ever since, people have reported hearing screaming coming from the woods and seeing hooded figures who chased away overly curious thrill seekers.

There are orbs and ectoplasm pictures that have been taken in the parking lot, but people can hardly ever take pictures near the tree, because their cameras malfunction. I get creeped out when I go there, and I refuse to set foot in the woods. I have heard of people feeling cold spots along the trails during the hottest days in July.

In 1995, Gerard John Schaefer was stabbed to death in prison.

If you're ever in the area, the park is located at 1982 S.W. Villanova Rd., Port St. Lucie.–*A.C.Y.*

The Haunt Oak

Just off the Old Dixie Highway north of Ormond Beach, next to the Bulow Sugar Mill ruins, stands the Haunt Oak. The big tree is also called the "Harwood Oak" or the "Fairchild Oak," the latter named for the botanist David Fairchild. There are two stories about this oak being haunted. One has it that a man was hanged there; according to the other, a former owner of the property, Norman Harwood, committed suicide beneath the oak in the 1870s.

Harwood did indeed die beneath the oak and was buried nearby in a coquina-rock vault. In later years, his body was exhumed and reburied in Atlanta, Georgia. His vacant vault was then used as part of a moonshine still and, later, as a pen for a pet alligator.

The Haunt Oak is said to be two thousand years old, but in reality it is about four hundred, which is old enough. With a spread of 133 feet, it is one of the largest oaks in Florida. Another weird and rare fact about this oak is that it's a "half-breed." David Fairchild classified it as a natural cross between a laurel oak and a live oak.

Where's Dead Man's Oak?

In Osceola County, there's a local legend about the Dead Man's Oak that has been passed down for generations and has found its way into a few ghost books, albeit with very little information. After receiving a few e-mails about this haunted tree, we decided to investigate and see if there was anything to it. The first version of this legend alleges that some Spaniards captured a man on a white horse in the vicinity of the Dead Man's Oak.

They strung him up and beheaded him beneath the tree for having committed a crime against the Spanish.

Supposedly, a headless horseman on a white horse can still be seen at midnight roaming around this old oak tree, and in some accounts he is said to be chasing people. The problem with this story is that this was hostile Indian territory during the Spanish period, and it seems highly unlikely that any Europeans, including Spaniards, or even criminals on the run would have been foolish enough to venture into these parts.

The second version tells of a man being hanged from the oak for cattle rustling, and it is his ghost that has been scaring folks, although in this case the phantom retains his head. Actually, this version has more historical credibility, since Osceola County has always been the heart of Florida's cattle country.

Depending on the source, the Dead Man's Oak is located about eighteen miles south of Kissimmee or about ten miles south of St. Cloud or two miles north of Canoe Creek or somewhere on the road to Kenansville.

The directions were not easy to follow, and to make matters worse, there are a couple of roads to Kenansville and thousands of oaks.

After a morning of driving and backtracking and having little success, we figured it was time to ask a local resident, a rancher leaning against a pickup loaded with hay bales. We pulled over and asked, "Have you ever heard of a tree called the Dead Man's Oak?"

To our surprise, he came back with, "You mean that hanging tree back up the road, where they say the ghost rider is?" He directed us back up the road to a lone oak tree standing in a pasture about fifty feet from the road. We took a photo of it, but it didn't look weird enough to us and certainly not old enough to have such a ghostly past. It appeared to be no more than seventy-five years old. Later we were directed to several other oaks, all masquerading as the Dead Man's Oak. Our conclusion is that nobody really knows its location, or maybe it no longer exists. Perhaps it never did exist, except in a persistent folk legend that still haunts imaginations.

Blame It on a Headless Horseman

Have you heard about the Dead Man's Oak Tree south of Kissimmee? They say there's a headless horseman that can be seen there at night. He is supposed to be the ghost of a man who got his head chopped off for stealing a horse.—*Ryan*

Chased by a Phantom

I can tell you that we used to drive by there on moonlight nights, and the only ghosts we ever saw was white cows. But I have a friend that I went to school with, and he heard about some kids who were driving by that oak tree, and they said they was chased by a phantom riding a horse. I think that is where the story comes from.—*Anonymous*

Where the Hell Is It?

I looked all over for the Deadman's Oak and can't find it. Nobody seems to know anything about it. Where the hell is it?—*firebox*

Blame It on the KKK

Go south of St. Cloud in Osceola County, and there is the Deadman Oak. That's where the KKK hung a man for stealing a horse. Nothing will grow underneath that tree. If you go by there when the moon is full, you can see a man hanging from the tree.—*alex*

XING

The Pathway of Wiccademous

In Fernandina, a scary legend has been making its rounds among teenagers for a long, long time. No one knows how old this story is, but according to local high school kids, it goes back at least a few hundred years. It has to do with an evil spirit called "Wiccademous" that lurks in the woods.

The story begins in the 1600s, when a young girl was brought to trial for practicing witchcraft and sentenced to be hanged. Her execution was carried out on September 12, 1600-and-something, the legend goes. No one seems to know the exact year, but for some reason, everyone claims to know the day and month.

Of course, there's a problem with this early date, since there wasn't much here in the 1600s, certainly not a village. No real settlements appear on any maps until 1767, when a town was established in the area of present-day Fernandina, and there are no records that suggest witchcraft was an issue here. Nevertheless, this legend of evil is rooted in witch-and-demon lore, hence the name "Wiccademous."

The location of the evil activity is across from the Fernandina High School, down a narrow path and under the branches of an ancient oak tree. It's here that Wiccademous will get you, say those in the know. The grave of the girl hanged for witchcraft is here, and if you dare to disturb it—that means just being near it—you'll feel the wrath of Wiccademous. Supposedly, the ground will shake violently, and you'll hear loud booming noises—all warnings for you to leave the area. Most of the time, these effects will be experienced before reaching the grave, but other times, the evil will let people get all the way there and then trap them. There are stories about how people have ventured into the woods and were never heard from again.

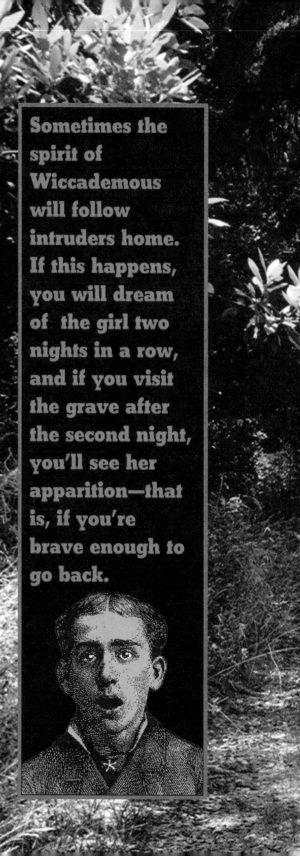

Sometimes the spirit of Wiccademous will follow intruders home. If this happens, you will dream of the girl two nights in a row, and if you visit the grave after the second night, you'll see her apparition—that is, if you're brave enough to go back.

She Believes in It

That's an old story; everybody at high school knew it. I don't know if it is true or not, but there is a big oak tree down that path. I believe in it because kids used to skip school and hang out there, and some of them said they saw things, but I never heard what they saw.—*Kathy M.*

The Body Down in the Ravine

The path is across from the new high school. You will see a sign that says something about a nature trail. The school used to use this for nature studies but for some strange reason has not used it in years. If you go all the way down this path, the ground will tremble because Wiccademous does not like people trespassing. There is a big deep ravine to the left of the trail, and Wiccademous has caused people to jump into this ravine. I don't know how true that is, but I know they found a body in that ravine a long time ago, before the school was built.—*Anonymous*

Demonic Energy That's Hundreds of Years Old

Hey, Wiccademous is real. It is an awesome force of demonic energy that projects itself in those woods. It is not new; it is hundreds of years old. That was where a coven of witches held meetings during the witch trials. I don't know if that witch part is true, but I know that there is something odd in those woods. I will not go around there.—*July77*

Grabbed by Wiccademous

That area is haunted by something. One time these boys I know were dared to go in there, and this was at night and I stayed by the car. They went in there, and they came running back and were really, really frightened and all out of breath. They made everybody get in the car, and we drove away real fast. They later told us that something grabbed them and held them, but they could not feel anything like a body; it was like it was invisible. I believe there is a Wiccademous.—*Kbar*

Tallahassee's Witch Grave

A century-old legend surrounds a curious tomb in Tallahassee's Old City Cemetery. As you enter the iron gates of the cemetery, you can't help noticing an ornate, towering obelisk marking a curious tomb. It's easy to get the feeling that this unusual grave magnetically beckons visitors to come closer. This is the most visited grave in the entire cemetery, mainly due to a legend about how it's the final resting place for a witch named Bessie.

"Bessie" is actually the nickname for Elizabeth Budd Graham, who was only twenty-three when she died in 1889, leaving behind a husband and two small children. She was laid to rest in one of Tallahassee's most elaborate tombs.

Surrounded by a stone wall, it includes large granite vases, a huge monument adorned with sculptured feathers, ivy, and a cross inside a crown. This was an expensive grave for 1889, considering that wooden markers were common at that time. Historians are not sure why Bessie rated such a fancy burial place, although there's a yarn about how she bewitched a wealthy man into marrying her.

The legend about Bessie being a witch is built around a number of odd things about her grave. To begin with, Bessie was born in October, the month of Halloween, and her grave is the only one in the cemetery that faces west, which some say is contrary to Christian burial custom. But it's the epitaph chiseled on her tomb that caused folks to conjure up a dark meaning. You'll probably recognize the passage from the mysterious Edgar Allan Poe poem "Lenore":

> AH! BROKEN IS THE GOLDEN BOWL:
> THE SPIRIT FLOWN FOREVER!
> LET THE BELL TOLL! A SAINTLY SOUL
> FLOATS ON THE STYGIAN RIVER;
> COME LET THE BURIAL RITE BE READ,
> THE FUNERAL SONG BE SUNG;
> AN ANTHEM FOR THE QUEENLIEST DEAD,
> THAT EVER DIED SO YOUNG,
> A DIRGE FOR HER THE DOUBLY DEAD
> IN THAT SHE DIED SO YOUNG.

Legend believers have deduced a variety of "witch evidence" from the epitaph. Some equate the first line, "Broken is the golden bowl," to driving a stake into a vampire. The lines "the spirit flown forever" and "a saintly soul floats on the Stygian river" are said to mean that a witch's spirit cannot cross the river of death and is trapped between life and death. According to certain practitioners of witchcraft who often visit the grave, the "Stygian River" is the Styx River of Greek mythology, where the souls of the dead were carried across the River Styx to the lower world. Others interpret "the queenliest dead" to mean she was the Queen of the Dead and "doubly dead" to mean a witch must be killed twice.

In spite of the allegations, we found no evil in Bessie's life. Maybe that's why most people will tell you that she was a "good witch." Good or bad, one thing is for certain: The strangeness surrounding her burial place has kept the spirit of Elizabeth "Bessie" Budd Graham alive for more than a hundred years.

Bessie Caught on Film

I belong to a group that investigates the paranormal in this part of Florida using various instruments that register EMF readings, temperatures, etc. On one full moon night following an electrical storm, we caught on a 35mm camera some orbs floating over Bessie's grave. They are definitely orbs just floating there above her grave.–*PHD*

Saw Witches at the Grave

When I was at FSU, a lot of the students would go to the cemetery at night just to see if they could see a ghost. One time we saw a group doing some kind of Wicca ritual with candles at this grave. It was a little scary, so we got out of there.–*Amy K.*

Mysterious Flowers at the Witch Grave

One of the most mysterious things that I heard about the so-called witch grave is that somebody has been placing flowers on that grave for over a hundred years and nobody knows who is doing it.–*Roger*

The Demon of Round Cypress

To find the site of this 1920s legend, you'll need a boat, snake-proof boots, and a healthy imagination. Down the St. Johns River in northwestern Seminole County, about halfway between Blue Springs and Lake Monroe, is a cypress head called "Round Cypress." For those who don't know much about cypress trees, a cypress head is just a stand of cypress trees. Cypress heads are usually a self-contained ecosystem, with taller trees reaching up for sunlight in the center and with smaller trees around the edge. We're not sure who named this place, probably early fishermen or moonshiners, but the name has almost faded away with the old-timers in this region.

According to local folklore, a demon or a witch—take your pick—resided in the darkness of Round Cypress. This evil entity was a shape-shifter, capable of taking on the form of any animal, in particular a bobtailed panther. Indeed, there was a bobtailed panther that roamed this region during the early '50s, and several old hunters have taken the credit for shooting off the big cat's tail.

In the 1930s, local boys were warned to stay away from Round Cypress, with tales about how some men were chased from their hunting camps by an unseen force that shook the trees, belched hot air, and made a loud growling noise. Other stories were told around campfires about how everything from ghosts to alligators lived in the sinister sanctuary of Round Cypress.

Weird Florida made a canoe journey down the river, landing within sight of it, and sloshed a short distance on foot through swampy saw grass and across a prairie to the sinister swamp. If there was something demonic about this place, we intended to encounter it for ourselves. The outside of this circular forest was bright and sunny, but inside, beneath the moss-draped, leafy canopy, it was eerily dark, with only a few patches of sunlight. Cypress knees were sticking up all over the place, which at a distance looked like short dark beings standing in the swamp. It looked like a perfect habitat for a demon. However, the only things we found were several pieces of rusted tin and some nice ceramic jugs, old bottles, and mason jars, all evidence of moonshining days. We wondered if the legends about demons and ghosts had been cooked up by the old whiskey makers just to keep nosy people away. If so, it would have been pretty effective.

Disappearing Fishermen

We were discussing local folklore at Halloween, and somebody was telling about a cypress swamp near Ft. Florida that is haunted. That is where an old woman lived who would invite fishermen into the woods, and they would not be seen again. You are supposed to be able to see this place from the river. It is almost perfectly round. Anyway, I thought it makes a good legend.–*Brenda J.*

Snakes Maybe, but No Demons

Round Cypress was a moonshiner's paradise during prohibition. You are liable to find anything in there, but I don't think there are any monsters or demons. Might be some snakes.–*oldbuck*

The Bobtailed Panther

There was a bobtailed panther that used to be seen in the northwest part of Seminole County, near the St. Johns. I know this for a fact because my dad used to hunt there and saw this cat several times around 1959.–*Jimmie H.*

Ancient Mysteries

it may come as a surprise to hear that Florida is part of northwest Africa, or so the theory goes. This mystery goes back eons ago, to our geological past, when North America was part of a supercontinent that included Africa. If the theory is correct, a rift split apart this huge landmass, with a fragment of North Africa becoming the base upon which the Florida and Bahamas platforms formed. Think about how weird this is. If that rift had not happened, there would be no Atlantic Ocean, and you could forget about vacationing at Daytona Beach.

Human migration to the Florida peninsula began when Peleo hunters arrived about twelve thousand years ago, at the end of the last ice age. We might add that air-conditioning was not needed in those days, since Florida's climate was cold and dry, much like that of the Arctic tundra. Most of the surface water was frozen in huge glaciers, which lowered sea levels, causing the peninsula to be fifty miles wider than it is today.

Very little is known about these ancient Floridians, because as the glaciers melted and sea levels rose, much of their remains were covered by water. But enough Paleolithic artifacts have been discovered to prove they were here. Several archaeological sites have been found at the bottom of Florida's springs and off the west coast, beneath the Gulf of Mexico. So don't be surprised if one day we find Atlantis off the east coast.

Florida had no organized communities until about 500 B.C., when early aboriginal tribes began building mounds along the rivers and coasts. Generally, the name "Seminole" pops up when we think of Florida Indians. That's because most people have never heard of Florida's vanished tribes, like the Ais, Timucua, Mayaca, Jeaga, Tequesta, Calusa, and Jororo. The Seminoles, originally part of the Creek Nation, didn't arrive until the early 1700s, well after the first Europeans.

Some history sleuths have spent years trying to piece together our histories and mysteries. This type of persistence led Florida's Mel Fisher to the lost Spanish treasure of the *Atocha*, which sank off Key West. We would all like to explore for lost treasure, but for now, let's be content with exploring a few of Florida's ancient mysteries.

Lake Okeechobee's Watery Graves

Lake Okeechobee covers 730 square miles of South Florida and parts of five counties, making it the second largest body of freshwater within the borders of the United States. The Calusa Indians called the great lake "Mayaimi," which is probably where Miami gets its name. In more modern times, it has been known as Lake Okeechobee, a Seminole word meaning "big water."

Lake Okeechobee has had its share of strange stories—tales about ghosts, lost treasures, and even monsters. In 1956, a pilot flying over the northern end of the lake reported seeing giant dinosaur tracks in the mud. Most of these weird accounts have been dismissed as just folk yarns. As for the dinosaur tracks, they turned out to be tracks left by dredging machines.

However, Lake Okeechobee has one bona fide unexplained mystery, with good physical evidence, that has baffled both scientists and local folk for many years: It's the secret of the Okeechobee bones.

Prior to 1910, early pioneers reported seeing human skeletons in the shallows around the southern end of the huge lake. Several old fishermen told of "catchin' human skulls" in their nets. One early settler claimed that there were so many skulls in the shallows that "during low water it looked like a pumpkin patch." A surveyor clearing land on the lake's Grassy Island in the early 1900s exposed more than fifty human skeletons that were covered with only a couple of inches of sand. This was not a case of dry land burials somehow drifting into the water. Grassy Island is not a natural island; it was originally lake bottom that was exposed when water levels were lowered by drainage canals.

Willis Crosby used to "catfish" in Lake Okeechobee, and he shared his story about finding a half-dozen human skulls in 1953 just lying in the mud on Observation Island. "There were a bunch of other bones scattered all over the bottom. I guess they were human," he reported. "Everybody said they were Indian bones."

All accounts of human bones come from the area extending from Kreamer Island to Observation Island. One theory is that these were victims of one of Okeechobee's terrible hurricanes. If so, then it would have been an ancient hurricane, because the two thousand dead from the 1926 and 1928 hurricanes were recovered and buried in mass graves on the mainland. Before

The Skeletons Were a Common Sight

I read about the skeletons they used to find in Lake Okeechobee. I live in Pahokee right on the lake and have heard the stories. It was a very common sight. The only place where these skeletons have been seen is on the south end of the lake.—*sugarcane314*

A Place of Ancient Human Sacrifices?

The bones of the lake are only visible during extreme low water periods. Has anyone considered that this may have been a place where sacrifices were made and over the hundreds of years the skeletons just piled up there?—*floridafolks*

1900, only a few people lived around Lake Okeechobee—certainly not enough to account for the estimated thousands of mysterious bodies on Okeechobee's bottom.

Some researchers have looked to the Seminole wars for answers to this mystery. However, the only local skirmish was the 1837 Battle of Okeechobee, on the north end of the lake, which resulted in only thirty dead. Historians have found no early Spanish connections to the mystery and believe that the bones may predate the first Spanish

Several old fishermen told of "catchin' human skulls."

period by thousands of years. Some speculate that the skeletons may have been those of residents of an ancient Indian village devastated by tribal warfare or disease. But if this is the case, what explains the total absence of artifacts and pottery?

Maybe the skeletons are the last

traces of a mythical lost tribe, like those mentioned in various religious chronicles. With the Florida peninsula extending so far south into the ocean, it's possible that ancient seafarers may have bumped into it at some time. Perhaps the skeletons belonged to refugees escaping from Atlantis. Until someone arrives with a good explanation for this ancient mystery of death, the secret will remain guarded by the big waters of Lake Okeechobee

New Smyrna's Mysterious Ruins

One tantalizing mystery on Florida's east coast is in New Smyrna's Old Fort Park, across from the city hall. Sitting on the east side of the park, facing the river, is what appears at first glance to be a ruined Spanish fort measuring forty by eighty feet. But was it a fort or something else? No one really knows.

Like the Castillo de San Marcos in St. Augustine, the ruins are constructed of coquina blocks, which would have required a considerable labor force and time. The project would have involved quarrying the coquina, cut-

Turnbull's wife, Gracia Dura Bin, was from Smyrna, Asia Minor, and so the settlement was named New Smyrna. Sailing in eight ships, 1,255 settlers survived a three-month journey, only to find extreme hardships awaiting them in Florida. First, preparations had been made for only five hundred people. Then there were the mosquitoes, heat, food shortages, Indians, and the difficult jobs of clearing land and digging drainage canals.

The colonists experienced harsh treatment by overseers, which resulted in rebellions and a dwindling labor force. Nine years later, only about five hundred souls remained in the settlement. Considering all of this, it

ting and shaping it, transporting it, and then building the structure. Who could have had such a labor force to build this fort, foundation, or whatever it is? There are no records to tell us.

According to local historian and publisher Gary Luther, the ruins have also been called the "Turnbull Ruins." In 1768, during Florida's British period, one Dr. Andrew Turnbull, a physician from Scotland, recruited 1,403 colonists to establish a settlement in Florida. Dr.

seems unlikely that these colonists had anything to do with building New Smyrna's weird structure.

There's another question that needs answering: Where was the quarry for the coquina rock used in the construction? If you calculate the number of coquina blocks that went into building this mystery, there would have to be a pretty big pit somewhere around town. In St. Augustine, the old Spanish quarries can still be seen on Anastasia Island, but no such pit exists in New Smyrna.

The ruins are not indicated on maps of the colonial period or mentioned in any records. However, on a map drawn in 1605, the Ais Indian village of Caparaca is shown at the location of the ruins. The ruins are believed to have been within a preexisting Indian shell mound

unfinished home? Perhaps Turnbull's palace? In 1778, following the collapse of the Smyrna colony, Andrew Turnbull moved his family to Charleston, South Carolina.

During the second Spanish period, which began in 1783, another doctor, Ambrose Hull, received a coloniza-

that was probably the village of Caparaca.

In his *History of New Smyrna*, Gary Luther writes that in 1776, a group of Englishmen from St. Augustine visited New Smyrna "to see the improvements, especially a very large stone building that was commenced for a mansion house." Luther adds, "Work was never completed because nearly all of the colonists, freed from their indentures, fled to St. Augustine in 1777." Does this mean that the ruins are the remains of a foundation for an

tion grant for 2,600 acres, including the site that is now Old Fort Park. By 1803, a new settlement had evolved at New Smyrna, with a population of five hundred to six hundred settlers. Hull referred to the location of the ruins as "Mount Olive" because of the olive trees that had been planted there by then. Although Hull offers no observations of any ruins at the site, he did write about having a number of stonemasons at work building a two-story house. Historians are in agreement that Ambrose Hull built his house on an existing foundation. But was it the foundation of the fort? No one is really sure.

We do know that in 1854, John D. Sheldon built a forty-room hotel and home on the site of the ruins. This building and another one later built on the site were both eventually destroyed. Now only the crumbling foundation of some structure remains, a silent reminder of people and times long gone.

Was New Smyrna, not St. Augustine, Florida's First City?

There is another intriguing, and controversial, mystery surrounding the New Smyrna ruins. The structure has very thick walls, making it considerably overengineered, unless it was intended to be a fort. The walls are three feet thick, with the same slope and workmanship as those in coastal Spanish forts.

This opens up a whole new can of worms. Was New Smyrna a Spanish settlement that predated St. Augustine? That's not so far-fetched when New Smyrna's other unexplained stone structures are brought into the picture. In addition to the ruins in Old Fort Park, there is the Spanish mission west of town. To the north, an ancient "Rock House" once watched over the inlet. According to John Detwiler, a local newspaper editor in 1887, there was a stone platform on a circular mound near the Rock House that looked like a gun traverse, a perfect spot for guarding the inlet with a cannon.

The Spanish mission, on Mission Road, is now a state park called the New Smyrna Sugar Mill Ruins. There is much debate about whether this was a mission or sugar mill. With all facts considered, it was probably a Spanish

mission that was later recycled as a sugar mill. There were actually three Spanish missions south of St. Augustine. The New Smyrna mission has window arches and architectural features similar to those in other Spanish missions, and some artifacts unearthed around its grounds also suggest a Spanish influence.

In 1925, editor Detwiler, a persistent man, spent a tidy sum of money trying to prove that New Smyrna was the first Spanish settlement in Florida. He went to Spain to look through the archives in Valencia, Madrid, Seville, and Toledo. The Spanish did, in fact, establish a settlement predating St. Augustine. Although no records have been found, the first settlement was described as "not having a harbor, not being visible from the ocean and subject to Indian attacks." Well, that sure sounds like New Smyrna. Detwiler believed that Spain's original settlement lasted about a year and may have been abandoned because of Indian hostilities.

More evidence is found in Ponce de León's log, in which he described landing where "four rivers formed a cross." Look at New Smyrna on the map and you'll see where Ponce de Leon Inlet and Spruce Creek intersect with the Halifax and Indian rivers to form a cross. St. Augustine has no such intersection of waterways.

Assuming that New Smyrna was the first Spanish settlement, why no mention, then, of the fort ruins in Turnbull's accounts or in those of the early traveler William Bartram? Gary Luther offers the possibility that the Spanish covered up the fort to prevent its use by adversaries, or perhaps the Indians covered it up to remove any traces of the Spanish.

New Smyrna's weird ruins remain a teasing puzzle waiting to be solved. Don't expect St. Augustine to give up its claim as the nation's oldest city, but there is a lingering question about the location of the very first Spanish settlement. Was it New Smyrna?

The Fountain of Youth Burial Grounds

When workers planting an orange grove in St. Augustine on April 13, 1934, uncovered human bones, they did not realize that the bones were part of an old Indian burial ground, dating to the time of Ponce de León's occupation. The site is now considered to be North America's first Christian Indian burial ground.

The bones of over one hundred skeletons, when excavated, were left in the exact positions they were found, and a building similar to that found in early Indian settlements was constructed over them. The remains were on exhibit in the Fountain of Youth National Archaeological Park until 1991, when the Timucua Indian Nation asked for them to be reburied.

Archaeologists have excavated the Fountain of Youth Park and have found many Indian artifacts, some predating Ponce de León's arrival by more than a thousand years. The park is the place where Spanish conquistadors first came ashore in what is now the continental United States. The Ponce de León expedition sighted land at what we now call St. Augustine. The Spanish called it "La Florida."

The Mysterious Miami Circle

The worst place in Florida to discover an ancient mystery is on prime real estate in downtown Miami. The Sunshine State has lost more historical sites to development than to any other cause. That's why local historians say, "When money talks, history walks."

In 1998, workers were demolishing an old Miami building on the south side of the Miami River to make way for a new high-rise condominium. To their surprise, they uncovered a thirty-eight-foot-diameter circular pattern of holes cut into the limestone bedrock. It was one of the greatest discoveries in Florida archaeology, but there was also a great big problem: The discovery was sitting on a $10 million piece of property that would be worth twenty times that amount if the two-acre site was developed into a condominium complex.

Archaeologists from Miami-Dade County's Historic Preservation Division examined the weird circle and determined that the holes were used to support posts for a large round council house. The circle was estimated to have been built between a thousand and two thousand years ago by the Tequesta Indians, who had died out centuries before the Seminoles migrated to the Florida peninsula.

Not everyone agreed with the findings, arguing that the circle was nothing more than the remains of an old septic tank and that the holes were overflow drain holes cut into the limestone. One man postulated that the pre-Columbian circle was part of a worldwide system of ancient circles that were somehow connected with Stonehenge. This theory caused some to dub the circle "Limestonehenge." Others claimed it was a sacred Mayan astronomical observatory for marking the passage of time. Opinions about the circle ranged from its having a connection to Atlantis to its being a corner marker for the

Bermuda Triangle. Media reports soon attracted New Age types, historians, Seminole Indians, shamans, spiritualists, and schoolkids, all wanting a glimpse of the ancient discovery or to experience its "supernatural qualities."

The Miami Circle was designated the Brickell Point archaeological site. It sits on land once owned by William Brickell, a pioneer who ran an early trading post. (William Brickell's weird mausoleum is nearby—weird because it is empty. When Miami began getting too crowded, Brickell's remains were removed by his descendants and reinterred in a Dade County cemetery.)

Excavating the ancient circle was not an easy task. Previously, six two-story apartment buildings and a swimming pool had occupied the property, and the ground was filled with rusty plumbing pipes, reinforcement steel, concrete, and other debris. After a tremendous amount of labor, the site was eventually cleared, exposing at least two hundred other postholes cut into the limestone in addition to the ones forming the strange circle. Other features that were uncovered included a carving of a large eye motif in the stone, twenty-four rectangular basins, a complete carapace of a sea turtle, a shark skeleton, and teeth from an extinct monk seal and a human. The most curious items were fragments of copper and galena, along with two small axeheads crafted from basalt. Since none of the artifacts are indigenous to Florida, this indicated that whichever early people inhabited the site, they had an extensive trade network two thousand years ago.

Several of the exotic artifacts led archaeologists to the conclusion that the site was used for ritualistic or elite ceremonial purposes. This was supported by the shark and turtle remains, which were found in what appeared to be an east–west orientation, perhaps deliberately placed for ceremonial reasons. A surveyor carefully calculated that solitary holes found forty-one feet on each side of the circle's center could predict the autumnal equinox and the summer and winter solstices. That piece of information added fuel to the theory that the circle was a Mayan-built giant astronomical calendar or some kind of almanac. And the eye motif carved in the limestone is the Mayan symbol for zero.

The idea that the circle was a Mayan project is not so far-fetched when you consider how close the Yucatán Peninsula is to the tip of Florida, and the Maya did, in fact, build seagoing canoes. It would have been easy for Mayan mariners to ride the Gulf Stream to Florida, although returning home might have been a problem.

The press played up the discoveries, which attracted so many people that the place had to be fenced off. For those who could not make it to Miami, a camera was affixed to the roof of a nearby high-rise to beam pictures to the Internet. The two-thousand-year-old circle had evolved into a kind of shrine, drawing attention from around the world.

Maybe there really was something magic about this circle. Save-the-circle groups held candlelight vigils, while protesters organized daily marches with signs demanding that the site be protected from development. Thousands of letters poured into government offices requesting action from local and state representatives. In October 2003, Senator Bob Graham introduced legislation that would authorize a feasibility study for incorporating the prehistoric site into Biscayne National Park.

Ultimately, Miami-Dade County, using the law of eminent domain, claimed the site. It was subsequently purchased for $26.7 million, funded by the state's Conservation and Recreational Lands Program, local contributions, and a loan from the Trust for Public Land. To preserve the area until more studies can be made, it has been covered with gravel.

The ancient people who once occupied this site could have never dreamed of the commotion their handiwork would stir up two thousand years later in downtown Miami or that images of their work would flash around the world on the Internet. Perhaps the weirdest part of the Miami Circle is how the ancient past has collided head-on with the present. Maybe the ancients have sent us a message in this circle. If so, we just have to figure out what it is.

It's a Sacred Place

The Miami Circle is a sacred place like Stonehenge. It is part of a celestial series of sacred places built by ancient people around the world. The circle itself is a spiritual symbol; we see it all over the world, even in crop circles. I know there is something to all of this circle stuff. I know it is history but someone needs to do some testing on the spiritual aspects of this religious place.–*lotusgem*

It's a Septic Place

I agree with James Randi, the great debunker of crap, who said that the circle is just a septic tank lid. Why do we waste so much money on this crap?–*budlite33*

Atlantis Connection?

The fact that it is right on the western boundary of where Edgar Cayce said Atlantis was, is it not possible that the survivors of Atlantis made it to Florida and joined with the Indian tribes there and formed the culture that made the circle?–*Anonymous*

Exciting Example of an Ancient Culture

The Miami Circle at Brickell Point is the most exciting example of ancient culture that I've seen in Florida. I think people need to get off their supernatural beliefs and see it for what it is, a great day for anthropology in Florida.–*Jim B.*

The Legendary Wakulla Volcano

It's a great mystery—that lonely smoke-pot in the vast Wakulla Swamp.

—*Maurice Thompson's* A Tallahassee Girl, *1881*

Twenty-five miles southeast of Tallahassee there's a secret buried in the vast Wacissa Swamp that's part of Florida's great pioneer legends. For nearly two centuries, stories have been handed down about the mysterious Wacissa Smoke, which supposedly came from the long-lost Wakulla Volcano.

The first accounts of the Wacissa Smoke can be found in early Seminole Indian lore that told of "smoke rising in the swamp." In 1830, settlers blamed the mystery on smoke from Indian campfires or from a pirate's den. The smoke varied from thick black, like coal smoke, to the bluish white of wood smoke and usually swirled upward, like smoke in a chimney, although it could be just a drifting haze. It was visible from far out on the Gulf of Mexico, and ships sailing into the port of St. Marks often relied on it as a navigational aid. Seafarers said it was "the old man of the swamp smoking his pipe." Superstitious folk claimed it was "the devil stirring his tar kiln."

The Wacissa Swamp is virtually an untouched wilderness dotted with numerous sulfur springs. Its subtropical growth covers a marsh that is the habitat of a variety of creatures, from snakes as big as your arm to a healthy population of gators. The only dry spots are a few pine hammocks. Many parts of this vine-tangled jungle are as inaccessible today as they were a century ago, which explains why very few people have ever tried to locate the origin of the smoke.

By 1840, Tallahassee residents were climbing up on rooftops to see what they thought was smoke from a camp of runaway slaves. On a clear day, the smoke could be seen from up to twenty miles away, and at night, people reported seeing a glow far out in the swamp. The *Tallahassee Patriot* described the glow in an 1880 article as "looking more like a large fire shooting its flaming tongue high up into the upper realms, frequently reflected back by passing clouds." During the Civil War, people speculated that the smoke was coming from a camp of deserters or from the mother of all moonshine stills. Each new theory seemed to ignore the fact that the smoke had been observed for at least a hundred years.

In the late 1800s, the *New York Herald Tribune* decided to investigate the situation, and an expedition was formed, made up of a New York journalist and three guides. They fought for nearly three days through saw grass, mud, mosquitoes, and cottonmouth moccasins but gave up their ill-fated quest after one of the guides fell out of a tree while trying to get a bearing on the smoke and the unfortunate New York reporter died from swamp fever.

Then the smoke suddenly ceased on August 31, 1886, when an earthquake hit Charleston, South Carolina, sending tremors throughout northern Florida. The legend lives on, but the smoke hasn't been seen since. Did the earthquake cause a geological effect that plugged up Florida's volcano? A recent inquiry to the University of Florida's geology department brought the following response: "We are unaware of the Wakulla Volcano as described, and certainly no volcanic activity occurred." But in recent times, numerous people have accidentally stumbled upon what they believed was the elusive crater. One old-timer described seeing "a blackened, dishpan-size hole atop a rocky knoll which was scattered with rocks." Others, including one William Wyatt in 1935, have claimed to find "scattered rocks that looked like they had been burnt by extreme heat." When Highway 98 was being built in 1949, workers came upon a deep hole in the middle of the Wacissa Swamp that required six hundred tons of rock to fill, hauled by thirty-four dump trucks. Was that the crater?

In October 1997, a team from UNX-Research, a nonprofit group investigating unexplained phenomena, went in search of the legendary volcano. The team, consisting of Jim Whitman and Bill and Todd Meyers, made their way by boat down the Wacissa River to where it meets the Aucilla River. According to most reports, the source of the smoke was near the intersection of these two rivers. "We hiked about two miles from the river to a high ridge that ran through a hammock," recounted Bill Meyers. "There was a high point on this ridge with rocks strewn everywhere. The rocks were overgrown with vegetation, but some were pretty large, at least a hundred pounds. Some of the smaller ones looked like they had been burned but we couldn't tell if it was because of a natural swamp fire or something else. We didn't find anything like a crater or anything that looked like lava material, and most of the rocks were plain ol' limestone or flint."

Over the years, people have offered numerous explanations for the mysterious smoke, but the swamp hasn't given up its secret. Somewhere out among the alligators and snakes lies the answer to Florida's lost-volcano mystery, perhaps waiting to become active again.

Weird Rocks in Rock Hammock

There's a place in the Wacissa called Rock Hammock. I've been there a bunch of times, and there's big rocks all over. They had to be pushed out of the ground by some kind of force, because I saw this for myself. *–Bryan G.*

Steam Coming from the Hole

My uncle used to hunt in those parts with a man that told him about a deep hole in a solid bed of rock that you could stick a large coffee can in, and he said that there was hot steam coming out of that hole. I heard there are underground caverns in that area. This makes me wonder if the Wakulla Volcano was really a hot spring. *–cyberhound*

Southwest Florida's Lost Treasure

Decipher the code, and you might find some of it.

Florida tops all other states in buried and sunken treasure, and only a fraction of it has been found. From Fernandina, at the tip of Florida, and up the Gulf coast to Pensacola, there could literally be billions in gold, silver, and jewels waiting to be discovered. As an example of what awaits the lucky treasure hunter, a cache of gold coins was found in the dunes of what is now the Canaveral National Seashore in 1969, and several years ago, while building a road in Brevard County, workers unearthed thirteen chests of coins. Spanish doubloons and pieces of eight have been found by beachcombers on Florida beaches after heavy storms. Some of this gold and silver washes ashore from ancient wrecks, but the buried loot most likely was hidden by pirates, like Black Caesar, Calico Jack, Morgan, Lafitte, and other ocean bandits who sailed under the black flag.

Pirates were not the only ones after gold and silver. Florida's early Indians salvaged treasure from the Spanish galleons whose unfortunate captains sank them in shallow waters or wrecked them on reefs along the coasts. We can only imagine how much treasure ended up "lost" in Florida.

The most famous Florida pirate was José Gaspar. Although some stories claim he was just a mythical character, there are accounts that lend evidence to the fact that he was a real person. Since 1904, Tampa has kept alive Florida's pirate past in its annual Gasparilla celebration. During the three-day event, a massive pirate ship, the *José Gaspar*, sails into Tampa's harbor and pirate reenactors invade the town. At 165 feet in length, with three 100-foot masts, the *José Gaspar* is considered the only fully rigged pirate ship in the world.

Gaspar, who also went by the name Gasparilla, was a saltwater scourge who, surprisingly, had been raised among Spanish aristocracy. He pulled off his first pirate stunt at the age of twelve, when he kidnapped a girl and held her for ransom. He was arrested and given the option of imprisonment or going to sea with the Royal Spanish Navy. Needless to say, he went to sea. He was later involved in a love affair with the king's daughter—that is, until she accused him of stealing the royal crown jewels.

With that, Gaspar decided to leave Spain, and in 1783, he began attacking any ship flying the Spanish flag. During his thirty-eight-year career as a pirate, Gaspar attacked over four hundred ships in the Gulf waters of Florida, including supposedly the vessel carrying $11.75 million in gold bullion that the United States had paid Napoleon for the Louisiana Purchase. If you find that hoard, just be advised that at last report, France is still seeking reimbursement from any treasure hunter who finds its gold.

Gaspar established his camp at the mouth of Charlotte Harbor. To add a little protection to his domain, he allowed another notorious buccaneer, Black Caesar, to build a camp to the south, on Sanibel Island. Gaspar not only took loot from ships, but also took women passengers to be his personal concubines. Those who were from wealthy families were put in a stockade on Captiva

mated that Gaspar himself had $30 million in treasure buried in thirteen chests and kegs within the vicinity of his camp. This does not include smaller caches buried by his crew, which numbered at least a hundred men.

During his thirty-eight-year career as a pirate, Gaspar attacked over four hundred ships in the Gulf waters of Florida, including supposedly the vessel carrying $11.75 million in gold bullion that the United States had paid Napoleon for the Louisiana Purchase.

The men were paid a share of the loot whenever a ship was plundered, and some of the small caches of coins found by treasure hunters probably belonged to individual crewmen.

Gaspar's reign as a pirate came to an end in the spring of 1822. He had planned to retire from pirating, but when his lookout spotted what looked like a helpless merchant vessel flying the British flag, Gaspar decided to plunder one more ship. It would be his last. He sailed out ready to take on the ship, but as he drew closer, he saw the British flag come down and the American flag rapidly hoisted up the main mast. He had been duped by the oldest pirate trick in the book. The ship was the U.S.S. *Enterprise*, a man-of-war vessel on a mission to put Gaspar out of business. Allegedly, Juan Gomez, one of the crew

Island and held for ransom. Some historians believe that is how Captiva Island got its name.

Gaspar and Black Caesar were buddies until 1817, when Gaspar found that Caesar had stolen some of his women. Gaspar attacked Caesar's camp on Sanibel Island, driving the rival pirate to Florida's Atlantic coast. Caesar did not have time to recover any of his buried loot on the west coast. Since Gaspar did not know where it was, we can assume that it is still there. It has been esti-

acting on Gaspar's orders, off-loaded treasure from the pirate ship into a long boat and with a team of men rowed for the shore and then up the Peace River. They set fire to the long boat but, because of the weight of the gold, had to leave some of the loot behind. The crew carried the rest of the treasure on their backs and buried it somewhere in the swamps along the Peace River.

In the meantime, back at sea, Gaspar, rather than risk capture and the hangman's noose, committed suicide by wrapping himself in an anchor chain and jumping overboard. His ship was hit with cannon fire and soon followed him to the bottom, along with an estimated $1 million worth of gold that was still on board. That loot is still on the bottom of the sea.

The last known living members of Gaspar's crew were Juan Gomez and Juan Gonzales. On July 12, 1900, Gomez drowned while fishing, having lived to the ripe old age of 122—or 120 or 119, depending on which story is to be believed. The *St. Augustine Record* reported that at the time of his death, Gomez was the "oldest man in the United States." The old salt was known for his tall tales of pirating, which many people did not really believe. However, a few years before his death, he told a story to a visiting journalist about a Spanish princess who was held by Gaspar. He said Gaspar had captured a ship with several women passengers, and in the group was a Spanish princess. As a captive, she became Gaspar's favorite even though she rejected his affections. The infamous pirate gave her an ultimatum—either submit or he would cut off her head. She rejected him one last time and was beheaded. Gomez sketched a crude map for his visitor showing where the princess was buried. A few years later, a grave was found at the exact location indicated on the map. In the grave was a headless female skeleton with a detached skull lying next to it.

As for Juan Gonzales, he continued pirating up to the Civil War, but age was catching up with him, so he settled down on Shell Creek near Lettuce Lake in De Soto County, where he lived for many years. He claimed to have been one of the crew that carried some of Gaspar's treasure up the Peace River, and said that a cask of it was buried on the shore of Lettuce Lake. After the Civil War, in the 1870s, the old pirate made a proposition to two ranchers, offering to cut them in for a share of the booty if they would help him dig it up and haul it. As agreed upon, the two men showed up at Gonzalez's cabin with a small boat on a wagon. Gonzalez told them that he was not feeling well and asked them to come back in a few days. When the two men returned, they found Gonzalez dead on the floor. After burying him, they searched the cabin and found a jar of gold coins and a small sheet of copper engraved with a code indicating the location of the treasure. The following is that mysterious code:

Since the 1870s, treasure hunters have been trying

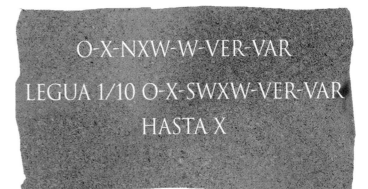

O-X-NXW-W-VER-VAR
LEGUA 1/10 O-X-SWXW-VER-VAR
HASTA X

unsuccessfully to crack this code, which some say is in Spanish. Others say it contains only compass bearings. The location is around Lettuce Lake. Decipher the code, and you might find some of Gaspar's lost treasure . . . but as fast as Florida changes, don't be surprised if you find a new shopping mall sitting square on top of it.

Fabled People and Places

Florida is a land of fact and fantasy, two ingredients that can stir up into one big myth featuring both fact and fantasy. This often results from a storyteller's embellishment or from an advocate of some weird tale trying to draw a flock of believers. There is never a shortage of believers, especially if there is a hint of truth to the story, which is usually the case. It is the tiny grains of fact that keep alive our folklore, fables, and even present-day conspiracy theories. All of us, at one time or another, have been duped into believing tales that turn out to be more fiction than fact.

Take the story about Sir Walter Raleigh laying his coat across a mud puddle so the Queen of England would not get her royal feet muddy. It is a romantic yarn of lost chivalry and a fateful meeting of two historical figures. The characters are factual, but the tale is fictional, invented in the 1600s by historian Thomas Fuller, who was known for adding a little spice to otherwise dull events. The story was then picked up by Sir Walter Scott and retold in his 1821 novel *Kenilworth*. It's a good example of a fiction supported with a little fact, embellished by a storyteller, and further advanced by a great author.

Sometimes places and people may be real but the beliefs surrounding them may not be. We know that Ponce de León landed in Florida, which is a real place, but what about the Fountain of Youth? Or a town called Two Egg? Do such places exist, and if they do, what are their stories?

Surprisingly, you'll find more facts than expected behind many of these places and people. But the best part is that you can visit most of the locations and see them for yourself, including the Fountain of Youth, if you can figure out which is the real one.

Cassadaga: A Town Founded by a Spirit

The quaint town of Cassadaga sits just off bustling Interstate 4 in Volusia County, yet it is one of the most peaceful places in central Florida. But what makes Cassadaga unusual is that every resident is a medium. That's right, spiritualism is the main industry here, aside from a couple of New Age bookstores, a café, a hotel, and a post office.

Cassadaga's history began in 1875, during a late-summer séance in Lake Mills, Iowa. It was there that George Colby, a twenty-seven-year-old medium, received a message from an Indian spirit named Seneca. Colby said that Seneca instructed him to leave Iowa immediately and make contact with T. D. Giddings, a medium in Eau Claire, Wisconsin. The two men were to conduct another séance, through which Seneca would commune with them. The two mediums complied with their orders and, while in a trancelike state, were told by Seneca that a congress of spirits had selected Florida for the establishment of a great spiritualist center and that Colby had been chosen to lead in its creation.

In a series of sessions that followed, Colby continued receiving directions from his spirit guide, Seneca. He was told that the proposed location of this new spiritual center would be "near Blue Springs, Florida, on high pine hills overlooking a chain of silvery lakes." It wasn't long before Colby and the entire Giddings family were moving to Blue Springs.

At first, the group resided in a palmetto hut to await further instructions. Then one night, in the faint light of a kerosene lamp, they were contacted by Seneca with orders to "go east, to the outskirts of the village and find the seven hills; this will be the place."

The next morning, they left Blue Springs. Near the town of present-day Lake Helen, they found seven pine-covered hills and saw the silvery lakes mentioned by Seneca. Both men agreed that this was the spot where they were to build a new spiritual center.

Cassadaga soon became looked upon as a strange place, where the devil's work was done. Backwoods preachers warned their congregations to "stay away" from Cassadaga, "lest ye be damned." This same feeling against spiritualism exists today, and residents still have hostile encounters with outsiders. "We've always had problems at Halloween," remarked Louis Gates, a certified medium and healer. "One time, they started a rumor that the devil was in the temple, because they could see a glowing red candle in the window. What they were talking about was the red exit lights inside the church. Then there are the stories about how we've dumped bodies into Spirit Pond." Gates says that these stories originate from people's ignorance about spiritualism. "If they understood it or could see it, they wouldn't fear it. . . . There's nothing evil about it."

THE DEVIL'S CHAIR OF CASSADAGA

Many of the original Cassadaga spiritualists are buried about a mile up the road in the Lake Helen cemetery. Each Halloween, guards must be posted at the cemetery to ward off outside pranksters and curiosity seekers looking for goblins. One of the big attractions at the cemetery has always been the sinister Devil's Chair.

According to the stories, if you sit in this big brick chair at midnight, the devil will communicate with you. The Prince of Darkness also enjoys a cold beer once in a while, for we're told that if you place an unopened can of beer on the chair, it will be empty the next morning. He's probably a pretty thirsty fellow after working in all that fire and brimstone.

Actually, there are three such brick chairs, so it is a little confusing trying to figure out which is El Diablo's. *Weird Florida* sat in all of them, but we didn't hear the devil say anything . . . maybe because we didn't leave him a beer.

When it comes to Cassadaga, Louis Gates is not only a medium, he's a regular historian and folklorist. He laughed as he began telling us the truth behind the legend. "There's nothing to it; kids started that story. The real story goes back to a man who lost his wife; it was a quick death and unexpected. This was back in the twenties. She was buried in the cemetery, and he

would walk there each day and sit beside her grave. The man had arthritis real bad in his legs, and the walk was hard on him. He needed something to sit on, so he built that big brick chair so he could rest beside his wife's grave. There are all kinds of stories, how if you sit in it, the devil will talk to you. . . . It's just a story. . . . It has nothing to do with the devil."

They Could Hear Voices

There is a big stone chair in Cassadaga. If you sit in this chair at midnight, the devil will talk to you. I know someone who went there, and they said they could hear voices in their head, but when they got up out of the chair, the voices went away. If you put a can of beer on the grave next to the chair, it will be empty in the morning and the top will still be sealed. Now how is that possible? But I know someone who did it, and the next morning, the can was empty.–*deathvader*

Dark Figures Lurking

Go to the Lake Helen cemetery just down the road two miles from Cassadaga. Up on the hill in the middle of the cemetery, you will see a large brick chair with arms. This is the Devil's Chair, and if you sit in it, he will appear. We went out there at night, but no one would sit in it because we saw some dark figures lurking in the shadows. We did not know if it was just some kids or something else.

–*thestetsonkid*

Weirdtown, U.S.A.

In Hillsborough County, on Highway 41 just ten miles south of Tampa, sits Gibsonton, once known as the strangest town in America. Called "Gibtown" by its nearly eight thousand residents, it has always been the retirement or wintering home of traveling showfolk. Call it "Showtown" or "Freaktown," Gibtown was the

final refuge for America's fading carnival culture. During the Depression, carnival and circus folks wintered in this part of Florida, with many of them parking their trailers in the off-season near the Alafia River. This was in the days of the big ten-in-one sideshows that featured live human oddities, like the Bearded Lady or Inferno the Fire Eater or the famous Grace McDaniels, the Mule-Face Woman. Today, sideshows are rarely found on carnival midways, which are now dominated by amusement rides and by game and food joints.

In Gibtown, your next-door neighbors might have been Priscilla the Monkey Girl, the Lobster Boy, or Dotty the Fat Lady. In other places, these strange people would have met with some degree of social rejection, but in Gibtown, they were treated as average people, bonded by the nomadic lifestyle of the traveling show.

In 1949, the famous Al Tomaini, an eight-and-a-half-foot-tall giant with a twenty-two-inch shoe size, retired from the road and settled in Gibsonton. The Giant and his two-foot-tall wife, Jeanie, billed as the "Half-Girl," started a trailer park and fishing camp that has become legendary among Tampa Bay fishermen as the Giant's Camp. Al and Jeanie Tomaini were known as the "World's Strangest Couple." For many years, Al served as Gibtown's police and fire chief. He continued operating his fish camp until his death in 1962.

In its glory days, Gibtown had the only post office in the country with a special low counter for midgets. The local fruit stand was operated by the famed Hilton Siamese twins, and down at the Showman's Lounge, the late Melvin Burkhart livened up the bar crowd by hammering six-inch spikes up his nose. Melvin was known on the road as a multitalented oddity, billed as the "Human Blockhead" and the "Rubber Faced Man."

In November 1992, Gibtown was hit with negative publicity when the Lobster Boy was murdered. The victim's real name was Grady Stiles, a member of the fourth generation in his family to be born with deformed hands that looked like claws and with legs that resembled flippers. Two of his four children inherited the strange genetic defect but were never exhibited on the sideshow stage.

Grady Stiles was married three times to two women. He drank too much and was frequently accused of abusing his family. Then, in November 1992, following years of misery, his wife, Mary Teresa, asked their son-in-law to help her escape from her husband. The solution was three shots in Stiles's head as he sat watching television in his trailer. The son-in-law was found guilty of murder and was handed a life term in prison. Mary Teresa was sentenced to twelve years.

Gibsonton is not the same as it was during the days of the big shows. Most of the famous freaks have died, but a few of their descendants still live there. As you drive through town on Highway 41, it looks like any other place, with a grocery store, gas station, library, and even a tattoo shop. But if you meander through the neighborhoods, the evidence is there. You'll see rusty parts left over from an amusement ride, a concession trailer, or perhaps an exotic animal. Gibtown has special zoning laws that allow such oddities to be kept on lawns. The Giant is long gone, the Half-Girl died in 1999 at age eighty-two, and you'll never hear the Fat Lady sing again. However, there is a strange nostalgia to Gibtown, especially if you like cotton candy, amusement rides, and weird exhibits, because this was home to those midway nomads who brought their special kind of fun to fairs and festivals across America.

During the Depression, carnival and circus folk wintered in this part of Florida with many of them parking their trailers in the off-season near the Alafia River. This was in the days of the big ten-in-one sideshows that featured live human oddities, like the Bearded Lady or Inferno the Fire Eater or the famous Grace McDaniels, the Mule-Face Woman.

MULE FACE WOMAN

ALIVE

It's Christmas All Year in Florida

If your idea of Christmas is snow, you won't find any here; as a matter of fact, the life expectancy of a snowman in this place is about an hour on a cool day. We're talking about the town of Christmas, Florida, located on State Road 50, halfway between Cocoa and Orlando.

Christmas residents may not have any snow, but they keep the happy holiday spirit all year long. At the main intersection in this small community is a permanent Nativity scene, and nearby is a big live Christmas tree that stays decorated all year. In keeping with the yuletide spirit, the streets have such names as Candy Cane, Frosty, Blitzen, Donner, Dasher, Rudolph, and Highway 50 East. . . . Oops, forget that last one.

The town takes its name from a stockade fort of the Second Seminole War period, which was built in December 1837. According to military records, the fort was opened on Christmas day but was occupied only a few weeks, which might give it the shortest occupation of any army post. A full-scale replica of Fort Christmas, which is also a museum, can be visited in the community's Christmas Park.

Most of the year, the town's post office operates at a normal pace. But just before Christmas, an avalanche of letters, cards, and packages is delivered to be remailed with the official Christmas postmark. This has been going on since 1930, when postmistress Juanita Tucker began stamping letters with GLORY TO GOD IN THE HIGHEST – CHRISTMAS ORANGE COUNTY, FLORIDA. Today, the Christmas post office offers a choice of postmarks, from Hanukkah to Kwanzaa to Christmas. Nobody gets left out. Of course, this has only increased business at the post office. Some letters don't come in for the postmark, but are addressed simply to Santa Claus. Maybe folks think that Santa, like so many other northerners, has retired to Florida.

You can see a display of these items all year at the post office, but if you plan to do any Christmas holiday mailings, you'd better get there early.

The Garden of Eden?

If you thought the Garden of Eden was somewhere in the Middle East, forget it. It was in Bristol, Florida—or so the legend goes. *Weird Florida* heard about this a few years ago and decided to check it out.

Bristol, located in Liberty County, looks like any other small town in northern Florida, except this was where Adam and Eve got their start, according to the late Elvy E. Callaway, a Baptist preacher in the 1950s. Sure, it sounds far-fetched, but hang on a moment: Reverend Callaway may have been onto something . . . or perhaps *on* something.

Callaway studied the area for fifty or more years and discovered a significant number of features that match the Bible's description of the Garden of Eden. He pointed

out that Genesis 2:10 states that "a river went out of Eden to water the garden; and from hence it was parted, and became into four heads." That sounds exactly like the Apalachicola River, which splits into four rivers. The reverend claimed that only two rivers in the world fit this description: one in Siberia, and the Apalachicola. We doubt that Eden was in Siberia; it's too cold there.

The Apalachicola River has cut a wide valley through this part of the state, where you'll find an impressive range of botanical species that grow in no other part of Florida, some in no other part of the world. Callaway identified twenty-eight kinds of trees here that are mentioned in the Bible. Of course, one might point out the absence of apple trees and demand to know where Eve got the apple that she ate. But advocates of the Garden of Eden theory point out that Genesis makes no mention of an apple. That's right—Eve ate from the tree of knowledge, and we're sure it's growing somewhere around Bristol.

In the early 1950s, the reverend's followers erected an entrance to the Garden of Eden and created nature trails through the woods and along the bluffs overlooking the Apalachicola River. In 1971, Callaway published his Eden theory in a book titled *In the Beginning.* The reverend died at the age of ninety-one, and as time went on, his Garden of Eden theory kind of fizzled out . . . but the Garden, or at least the woods, is still there.

Today, the area is owned and managed by the Nature Conservancy. The entrance is marked by a small sign that makes no mention of the Garden of Eden, and around it is only high dry scrub of sand pines, turkey oaks, and palmetto bushes. It certainly doesn't look like the Bible's version of the Garden of Eden. But hike a winding trail for about fifteen minutes, and the sandhill pinelands give way to a lush forest of beeches, magnolias, dogwoods, hollies, and laurels. A narrow path trails along the edge of a deep ravine, its slopes covered with ferns and laced with purple flowers of wisteria and white dogwood blossoms. Butterflies flit over a crystal-clear stream of water. The place really does look like a natural garden.

Eventually the trail comes out to a bluff overlooking the Apalachicola. Nothing about this landscape looks like Florida. The soil is reddish clay, the kind Native Americans used to make pottery. Could this have been the dust used to create Adam?

Weird Florida can't say for sure if Elvy Callaway's theory was correct, but in county records, the description for this property is "The Garden of Eden Tract." Guess that really does make it the Garden of Eden.

The She-Man of the Caloosahatchee River

There's a rather persistent tale in South Florida folklore about a hermitlike character called the "She-Man," who roamed the banks of the Caloosahatchee River, which stretches from Lake Okeechobee to Cape Coral on the Gulf Coast. There is a problem in trying to date the events in this folk yarn, which some say happened prior to 1900, while others claim it was in the 1920s.

The She-Man, according to those who allegedly knew him (apparently it was a him, despite the name), was a reclusive fellow who had gone bonkers and preferred to avoid civilized folks.

In their campfire accounts, hunters often recalled how the She-Man always wore a woman's dress

The She-Man, according to those who allegedly knew him, was a reclusive fellow who had gone bonkers and preferred to avoid civilized folk.

and had a pet alligator that followed him around like a dog. The man would run along the banks of the river, keeping a sharp eye on anyone passing through his domain in a boat. Fishermen said he would spy on them from behind cypress trees, and if spotted, he would quickly vanish into the swamp. People said he "knew the swamp better than any Seminole."

There are several stories concerning the She-Man's identity and how he came to live so far from civilization. The most popular version, which has developed into a folk legend, is that the man went insane after his family was killed. According to that legend, he had lived with his wife and son in a cabin rented from his employer, a Mr. Morgan. The story does not tell us what kind of work he was engaged in, but alleges that Morgan was a direct descendant of the notorious pirate Captain John Morgan and knew about some buried treasure.

At some point in time, the man's wife and son were out in the swamp and came upon Morgan burying a treasure chest. Morgan, knowing he had been discovered, hit the son over the head with a shovel and threw his body into the hole with the chest.

The wife ran for her life, with Morgan fast on her trail. Her husband later found her beaten and dying on a path in the swamp. Before she died, she managed to tell her story, which sent her husband into a rage. He donned her clothes and became the fabled She-Man of the Caloosahatchee.

Now demented, the creature wasted no time in avenging the murder of his family. Along with his pet alligator, named Devil, he found Morgan making his getaway in a rowboat. The She-Man jumped into the water and overturned the boat, spilling Morgan into the jaws of ol' Devil. After that, the creature continued to live a reclusive life deep in the swamp, emerging only to watch for any intruders. Today, only the fable remains.

Is it a true story? No historical records have been found to substantiate the facts or prove that the characters even existed. Folk historians *Weird Florida* have spoken to believe it is just folklore. Some people along the Okeechobee have heard the tale, but none have seen the poor he/she critter.

But there could be just that grain of truth in it. Perhaps a hermit really did inhabit the swamp sometime in the dim past, flitting among the cypress trees, keeping a wary eye on intruders. No doubt yarn spinners have added their own ingredients to enhance the tale, and thus another Florida legend is born.

Cyrus Teed's Shocking Revelation and Hollow-earth Settlement

If you're looking for the center of the universe, look no farther than the Estero River, just south of Fort Myers in Lee County. This is the spot where Dr. Cyrus Reed Teed established his Koreshan Unity Settlement, an unusual colony of hollow-earth followers.

Cyrus Teed, who was born in 1839 near Trout Creek, New York, spent his younger years experimenting with alchemy and electrical phenomena and studying medicine. He became a doctor but continued with his electrical experiments well into adulthood.

In one of those experiments, he received a severe jolt that knocked him out. While unconscious, he claimed to have experienced a divine illumination. (We can believe that: Just receive a surge of electricity, and you'll be illuminated too.) Teed said that during this spiritual awakening, a beautiful woman revealed the secrets of the universe to him and told him that he had a mission to "redeem humanity."

Following his "shocking experience," Cyrus Teed's theories began getting a little strange. He changed his name to Koresh (pronounced ker-ESH), a Hebrew name taken from the Book of Isaiah 44:28. Then he began promoting a pseudoscientific notion that the earth is a hollow spinning sphere and that we inhabit the inside, held to the inner walls by centrifugal force. Actually, Teed hypothesized that the entire universe was contained inside a supersized womb, called "Earth," with the planets and sun suspended in the center, except the moon, which Teed said was just an illusion.

Teed's beliefs were based on what he called "Cellular Cosmogony," a distorted mixture of science and religion. He said that he had discovered the "vitellus of the great

cosmogonic egg." Translated, that means he had found the belly button of the earth, the epicenter of the Second Coming of Christ, which he calculated to be near Fort Myers, Florida.

Teed's theory was appealing to many religious fundamentalists because it meant that the earth was not just another tiny speck in the universe. It contained the whole works inside, and there was absolutely nothing on the outside.

What is even weirder than Teed's theory is that he was able to recruit a large number of educated people for what he called the "Koreshan Unity." In 1894, they acquired 320 acres of land on the Estero River and set about building a utopian settlement called New Jerusalem. Koreshan-style socialism advocated communal living, sexual equality, and celibacy. Though its followers strongly opposed being slaves to a wage-earning society, they were self-sustained by a keen sense of business, and the settlement rapidly evolved into a prosperous community that included several flourishing enterprises.

Earthly success aside, most people thought Teed was off his rocker, and he was even sued in court a few times for trying to raise funds by claiming to be the second Christ. To recruit more members and convince his pesky skeptics of his theories, he called on Professor Ulysses Grant Morrow of the Koreshan College of Life to come up with an experiment to show, once and for all, that we all live inside the earth.

To prove Teed's strange theory, Professor Morrow devised an instrument that he dubbed the "rectilineator," which would measure the curvature of the earth. The weird contraption consisted of ten huge double T squares made of seasoned mahogany, set horizontally on ten carefully balanced mounts.

In January 1897, Professor Morrow and a dozen followers worked for nearly a month to set up and calibrate the big apparatus on a stretch of beach at Naples, Florida. If the experiment worked, it would show that the earth's surface curved upward at the rate of eight inches per mile. Morrow projected a horizontal line westward. If his calculations were correct, this reference line would meet the water about four miles offshore in

the Gulf of Mexico, thus proving a concave surface. On the other hand, the rectilineator would also indicate if the earth's surface was flat or convex.

Since the contraption was only twelve feet long, it had to be moved and calibrated section by section in order to repeat the crazy experiment over the four-mile distance. It took five months, but on May 5, 1897, Teed announced that the end of the instrument had touched the water just where he said it would, proving that we live on the inside of the earth. Needless to say, the experiment has had no revolutionary impact on conventional science. However, the Nazis, in their attempt to control the world, checked out several strange occult claims, including Cyrus Teed's hollow-earth theory. If by some remote chance Teed was correct, then they would be able to spy on the United States by pointing a telescope up. According to several unconfirmed reports, a secret group of Nazi scientists briefly evaluated Teed's far-fetched idea before tossing it out.

In 1904, 110 acres of the Koreshan Unity settlement were incorporated as the town of Estero. But the prejudice of local folks who did not like the Koreshan's communistic lifestyle led to many confrontations. Teed was injured in one of these altercations, and the Koreshans maintained that the injury led to his death on December 22, 1908. Teed had told his followers that he was immortal and that upon his death he would be resurrected. Koreshan members held on to his body until after Christmas, but nothing happened, and the coroner finally ordered that the body be buried.

Cyrus Teed's failure to rise from the grave proved to be a great disappointment and led to the downfall of the Koreshan community. The younger members began drifting away, and those who remained split up into factions over the struggle of who would succeed Teed. Most of the 250,000 historical records documenting Koreshan history have been kept at the Koreshan College of Life Foundation museum. Few outsiders, including state archivists and historians, have seen this loosely organized historical collection. The foundation is still active. However, the original three-hundred-acre site of Cyrus Teed's utopian community is now owned by the state of Florida and is listed on the National Register of Historic Places as the "Koreshan Unity Settlement Historic District." So in some sense, the community lives on.

Florida's Fabled Fountain of Youth Springs Eternal

No book about Florida's fabled places would be complete without mentioning Ponce de León's quest for the Fountain of Youth. We are not talking about St. Augustine's Fountain of Youth here. You know the place—that tourist attraction where after you pay admission, they give you a paper cup so you can drink from the rejuvenating spring. Does anyone ever feel different after drinking from that spring?

There are several other springs in Florida claiming to be the real Fountain of Youth, including two Ponce de León springs. That's right, there are two Ponce de León springs: one north of Deland in Volusia County and the other just off I-10 in Holmes County. There are also six mineral springs in Safety Harbor that claim to be the mythical fountain.

The Fountain of Youth was not Ponce de León's primary objective when he landed in Florida. He was looking to find gold and to claim lands for Spain. That's not to say that he hadn't heard of this spring of rejuvenating water, because stories of such a place had long circulated in the Spanish court. Ponce de León was thirty-nine years old when he arrived here.

JUAN PONCE DE LEÓN

AT THE FOUNTAIN OF YOUTH

Spanish historian Francisco Lopez de Gomara wrote in his journal that Indians living on the island of Hispaniola had told him about a fountain with healing waters north of Cuba and Haiti. The Indians usually referred to this mystical place as a river, waterfall, or spring. It was the Spanish who added the word "fountain." Some of the facts about this miracle water source may have been misinterpreted in the translation from the native tongues to Spanish. Were the Indians simply referring to springs where exploring conquistadors could obtain fresh drinking water? After all, water sustains life. Without water, life can be rather short, and with it, life will certainly be longer.

Several years ago, *Weird Florida* interviewed a member of a secret society in St. Augustine who claimed to know the true location of the elusive Fountain of Youth. This society is so secret that even its name cannot be revealed. According to the informant, who said he was ninety-three years old but looked forty, it was founded prior to 1845, the year Florida gained its statehood. Members of this secret order are sworn to protect the fountain from disclosure. Knowledge about the spring was allegedly passed down through a St. Augustine family of British-Spanish descent. As proof, our anonymous source offered copies of census records of members who had lived beyond 110 years, including Juan Gomez of Panther Key, who drowned at the age of somewhere between 119 and 122.

We pointed out to our mysterious source that drinking from the fountain must have done no good, since they were all dead. He responded by saying that all had been killed or drowned. None had died of old age. We checked his records again, and he was correct. So even if you do drink from the Fountain of Youth, it won't pro-tect you from getting hit by a tour bus from New Jersey.

There is really no evidence that Ponce de León ever found the Fountain of Youth. But is it entirely a fable? Florida has more springs than any other state, including Wakulla Springs, which means "place of mystery waters." At two hundred feet, Wakulla is the deepest spring in the world. The most beautiful is Silver Springs, near Ocala. Ancient people living around Silver Springs referred to it as "Sua-ille-aha," which vaguely translates as "sun-glittering waters." It was considered a sacred place of "life-giving water." In 1856, anthropologist Daniel Brinton explored Silver Springs and wrote of the early Indians "spreading the fame of this marvelous fountain to far distant climes, and under the stereoscopic power of time and distance came to regard it as the life giving stream, whose magic waters washed away the calamities of age and pains of disease, round whose shores youths and maidens ever sported young and eternally joyous."

Florida's springs are indeed life-giving. Not only is the crystal-clear water from these springs life sustaining, but there is an abundance of nutrients necessary for maintaining good health. Here's a partial list of rejuvenating trace nutrients found in Florida's springs: carbonates, boron, chromium, copper, gold, iodine, manganese, nickel, fluoride, sea salt, zinc, sulfates, sulfur, iron, and magnesium.

So maybe there is some truth to this Fountain of Youth story. Just look at all the senior citizens living life to its fullest in Florida. When native Floridian Mary Thompson died in July 1996, she was 120 years old and held the honor of being America's oldest person. With evidence like this, maybe Florida really does have a Fountain of Youth.

The Coral Castle

It's been called Florida's Stonehenge, a massive rock structure on the Dixie Highway, north of Homestead. The mystery of this strange place is really about its builder, Edward Leedskalnin. A small man who stood only five feet tall and never weighed more than a hundred pounds, Ed accomplished an unbelievable, perhaps even supernatural, feat of engineering that is still a baffling mystery.

Ed Leedskalnin's heartbreaking story begins in Riga, Latvia, where he was born in 1887. On the day before he was to wed his sixteen-year-old fiancée, Agnes Scuffs, she had a change of heart. It was a jilting that would haunt Ed for the rest of his life. He left his country and wandered through Europe and Canada, before finally coming to South Florida in 1918, where he bought some land in Florida City.

Once he was settled in his new home, Ed went about carving massive blocks of coral stone into a monument to his lost love—a kind of rock palace. The little man quarried and transported the huge blocks, many weighing several tons, to the shrine he was building, then carved and put them in place. Most of his work was done secretly at night using only basic tools, such as iron wedges, saws, block and tackle, and a wagon. He had no engines or power source other than himself to move and position more than 1,100 tons of coral rock. The tallest structure in his rock palace is a tower containing 243 tons of stone, with the average block weighing 9 tons. There is an obelisk weighing 28 tons. The heaviest stone object weighs 35 tons.

No one really knows how such a small man was able to accomplish such a monumental task or why he worked under the cover of night. During the day, Ed would rest or study his books on cosmic energy and magnetics. He had a keen interest in science, astronomy, and the Egyptians, in particular the pyramids. Whenever people asked him how he moved the mammoth blocks of stone, he would only reply that he had discovered the secrets of levitation used in building the pyramids.

As if there was not enough weirdness surrounding Ed's project, when Florida City became too crowded for his liking, he dismantled his massive work in 1936 and moved it down the road to Homestead. He borrowed a friend's tractor and truck and began the superhuman task of loading, unloading, and reconstructing his rock castle on ten acres of land, where it still stands today.

According to one story, a few curious folk decided to spy on Ed to see how he moved the heavy stones. They claimed that he placed his hands on each stone and began chanting and that the stones would somehow float up into place. No one understood it.

There are many theories about how this frail man could have moved so many tons of rock. He himself disagreed with modern science, saying it was all wrong when it came to magnetism and gravity. Ed believed that all matter consists of individual magnets and that it is the movement of these magnets within matter and through space that produces magnetism and electricity. He claimed that his concepts involved the relationship of the earth to celestial alignments and that he could actually see particles of light that were the physical presence of natural magnetism and the life force.

The phenomenon Ed was referring to is known in Chinese medicine as "chi." A New Zealand airline pilot decided to study Ed's claims and found that, based on the geographical location's longitude and latitude, Ed had selected the right spot on the planet for producing "the geometric harmonics necessary for the manipulation of anti-gravity." In other words, if Ed was going to levitate something, he picked the perfect place to do it.

On the other hand, maybe he was just a superclever guy who figured out new ways of using levers and block and tackle. But then we have the problem of trying to figure out where he got ropes strong enough to hold all that tonnage.

At the new location, the amazing Stonehenge-like structure was called "Rock Gate Park." It actually looked more like a gigantic rock home, surrounded by a heavy stone wall with a tall tower sticking up in one corner. Inside, there were massive stones carved into huge chairs and tables, an outdoor bathtub, a giant table in the shape of Florida, a fountain shaped like the moon, stone beds and pillows, a rock telescope, and big superheavy stone gates. In 1986, when one of the nine-ton gates needed repairs, it took six men and a fifty-ton crane to move it. Yet little Ed Leedskalnin, without mechanical assistance, had moved, positioned, and precisely balanced the gate so that a mere child's finger would push it open!

Ed Leedskalnin never gave up hope that his long-lost love would someday join him at his estate of stone. It was never to be. Ed died in 1951, still without his beloved Agnes. After his death, Rock Gate Park passed to his nephew. In 1953, it was sold to private owners and renamed Coral Castle.

In 1992, when Hurricane Andrew wiped out most of South Florida, Coral Castle stood like a stone fortress. Today, it is open to the public as a curious stone marvel, preserving forever the legacy of Edward Leedskalnin.

Unscrambling the Town Name of "Two Egg"

The most stolen city sign in Florida is not the one for Orlando or Miami; it's the sign for the town of Two Egg, a pleasant rural community in Jackson County. This sign was stolen so many times that the highway department had to use extra bolts to affix it to the frame. But this did not stop the poachers; they began cutting off the pole at the base.

Fed up with replacing the sign, the state eventually moved it closer to town so folk could keep an eye on it. The unusual name has put Two Egg in the pages of several national and regional publications, including a 1982 mention in *National Geographic.* It's even found its way into a couple of television travel documentaries. But please note, Two Egg is really two eggs times one. In other words, there's no *s*; it's just plain "Two Egg."

Local residents are fond of saying, "If you blink, you'll miss Two Egg." When *Weird Florida* visited, local Two Eggian Nell King was gracious enough to talk about the town's history. Nell operates the Lawrence Grocery, a nostalgic general store with two gas pumps. It's the kind of down-South store where you feel a little sacrilegious if you don't buy yourself a Moon Pie. Across the street is another old store, which has been closed for so many years that the gas pump

is still stuck on twenty-nine cents a gallon. This is the middle of "downtown" Two Egg, Florida.

Our main purpose for coming to town was to find out how Two Egg got its name. "Well, there's several stories about where the name Two Egg came from," explained Nell King, who is the unofficial tourist bureau for Two Egg. "Originally, this place was called Allison, a sawmill town back in the 1800s. One theory is that somebody dropped two eggs in the road and changed the name. Another story has it that the first thing sold at the old country store was two eggs, and there's yet another one, about a woman sending a child to the store with two eggs to trade for a weasel of snuff.

"But the one that is best accepted is about a man named Will Williams. He had fifty-seven children by three wives [or fifty-six or forty-six, depending on the story]. Mr. Williams had even more chickens than he did children. This was during hard times, when money was short, and Mr. Williams would send his kids down to the store with eggs to barter for something. One day, a traveling salesman was in the store and saw the children trade two eggs for candy. The salesman said, 'We'll just call this place Two Egg.' That is the most accepted story about how the town got its name."

There are plenty of other theories to go around, but if you visit Two Egg, please don't steal their sign. Instead, buy a Moon Pie and a genuine Two Egg souvenir at the general store.

Unexplained Phenomena

The universe is a place filled with weirdness, and what mysteries science has been able to solve, even with all our present-day knowledge, would fit on the head of a pin. The rest remains shoved into the file drawer marked "UNEXPLAINED PHENOMENA."

This chapter is about the UFOs, strange disappearances, weird lights, ESP, and anything downright paranormal that has appeared on our sunny peninsula. Sometimes we label these things "supernatural," a word used to describe anything beyond what science considers "natural." (Of course, if we could go back in time and demonstrate a computer to the folks at Salem, we would probably be charged with practicing witchcraft. What was considered supernatural yesterday may be perfectly natural today.)

The unexplained cannot be witnessed by all of us, so we are left to judge the testimony of others. Certainly there are misinterpretations and hoaxes, but what about credible witnesses who report incredible experiences for which we have no explanations? On second thought, if we explained all of this weirdness, we'd take the fun out of it. In that respect, maybe some mysteries are best left unsolved and unexplained.

Human Incineration in St. Petersburg

One of the most baffling of all unexplained phenomena is SHC, or spontaneous human combustion. This is when the human body or some part of it suddenly bursts into flames. In many cases, the body is totally reduced to ashes by intense burning but with little or no heat damage to surrounding objects. Reports of SHC go back hundreds of years, with several accounts appearing in seventeenth-century medical journals. Charles Dickens wrote about it in his novel *Bleak House,* in which he describes the death of a villainous character named Krook.

His charred remains are discovered in his squalid room. . . . There is a smouldering suffocating vapor in the room, and a dark greasy coating on the walls and ceiling. Call the death by any name . . . it is the same death eternally—inborn, inbred, engendered in the corrupted humours of the vicious body itself . . . Spontaneous Combustion.

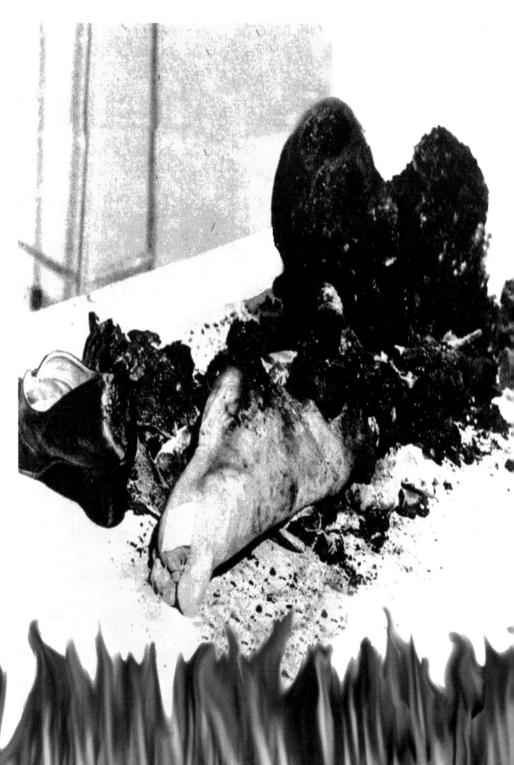

Skeptics refuse to believe that the human body can incinerate itself, but for a moment, let's consider some facts. We humans stuff all kinds of flammables into our systems: alcohol, fats, certain medications, and gas-producing foods. Beware of beans—intestinal gases can be like methane gas produced by decaying biomass. And look at the biological makeup of the human body. It contains large amounts of fat, oil, phosphorus, and other substances that will burn. Any cook can attest to the persistence of a grease fire in the kitchen. We also consume large quantities of oxygen, which is needed to sustain both life and fire. Add in a fact from the *Fire Protection Manual,* which states that the human body can accumulate several thousand volts of static electricity. Considering all this, we could be walking combustibles just waiting for ignition.

One of the world's best-documented cases of SHC is that of Mary Reeser, sixty-seven, of St. Petersburg, Florida. On the morning of July 2, 1951, her landlady went to Mrs. Reeser's apartment to deliver a telegram and found the door handle extremely hot. Fearing that the apartment was on fire, she yelled for help. Hearing the landlady's pleas, two painters working next door ran to her aid. They opened the door and were hit with a rush of hot air. The two men immediately went inside to rescue Mrs. Reeser, but she was nowhere to be found. Strangely, there was only a little smoke coming from a small flame burning on a wooden beam separating the kitchen from the living room.

The fire department arrived and quickly extinguished the flame, but there were still no signs of the sixty-seven-year-old tenant. When Fire Chief S. O. Griffith came on the scene, he was shocked by what he found. In the middle of the floor was a four-foot-square scorched spot with the remnants of a chair and the incinerated remains of a human body. Mrs. Reeser had been reduced to a pile of ashes, except for her skull and one foot, which was still in its slipper.

An investigation was launched involving the police, state fire marshal, arson experts, pathologists, and even an FBI agent. The experts were left puzzled—there seemed to be no heat damage beyond the four-foot area containing the victim's ashes. The ceiling directly over the burned area was coated with oily soot like that produced by a grease fire. Close by were flammable items: newspapers and linens. However, all were untouched by the heat.

The investigation ruled out lightning, electrical malfunctions, smoking, and all other likely causes. It appeared that Mrs. Reeser had simply exploded into flames and burned up. The fire experts estimated that the temperature must have been three thousand degrees in the room, yet there was little heat damage. The final conclusion was that Mrs. Reeser had died from a fire of unknown origin. The official report referred to the incident as "unusual and improbable."

iami's Famous Poltergeist Case

The word is German, and it basically means "noisy ghost." We've all heard haunted-house stories about objects flying off shelves, levitating furniture, rapping sounds, or lights mysteriously turning off and on. Most parapsychologists put such events into the realm of poltergeist activity, which may be caused by psychokinetic energy projected by a living person rather than a spirit. Poltergeist incidents, with few exceptions, have usually involved adolescents experiencing physical or emotional turmoil in their lives. One of the best-documented poltergeist cases happened at the Tropication

The unexplained antics continued to get worse, and by January 1967, the workers were in a state of panic. The owners decided to call in the police to investigate.

During the first hour they were there, police officers observed the phenomenon for themselves and called for a backup squad to help figure out what was causing it. Insurance investigators came in to determine the cause of the damage. Like the others, they were mystified by what they saw.

Unable to explain the activity, the police contacted the American Society for Psychical Research. After spending ten days studying the situation and documenting 150 poltergeist incidents, researchers determined it was not a hoax. They also discovered that a certain Cuban teenage

Arts warehouse, a Florida souvenir-and-novelty supplier in Miami.

The shenanigans began on December 15, 1966, when several glass objects and ceramic mugs were found broken. Soon workers began seeing items rolling off shelves by themselves. They saw boxes flying from one shelf to another, often missing an employee's head by inches.

boy, Julio Vasquez, was present during each poltergeist occurrence. Vasquez, nineteen, had been experiencing personal problems, and researchers theorized that that might have contributed to the poltergeist activity. This theory was bolstered when all such activity ceased on January 30, 1967, the same day management fired Vasquez for taking petty cash.

The shenanigans began on December 15, 1966, when several glass objects and ceramic mugs were found broken. Soon workers began seeing items rolling off shelves by themselves.

Vasquez was asked by the American Society for Psychical Research to undergo some tests to determine if he possessed psychic abilities. The experiments suggested that the young man had a remarkable potential for producing psychokinetic energy. The research foundation wanted to do more testing at the Durham Technical Institute, but Vasquez declined, saying he did not feel like being a guinea pig for science.

There were 225 poltergeist incidents documented in this case, much of it personally observed by employees, police officers, insurance investigators, a magician, news reporters, and parapsychologists. The police record is detailed but offers no explanation . . . other than that it was poltergeist activity.

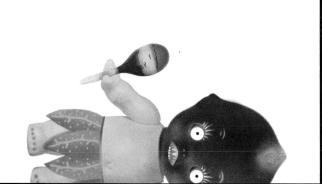

Tomoka's Carnivorous Pink Cloud in the Woods

Between 1955 and 1966, several people reported encountering a strange pink cloud that hung low to the ground in the woods along the Tomoka River, west of Daytona. For years, local kids had told of a strange globe of light that would chase cars on Tomoka Road, but this light doesn't seem related to the cloud. Usually, the cloud was seen in the cooler months by hunters and, on at least one occasion, by a fisherman on the Tomoka River. It seems plausible that fog would hug the ground in cooler weather and, with the right sunlight, might reflect a pinkish tinge.

The first explanation that comes to mind is that this was some kind of chemical pollution, except that in those days the area was rural, without any industrial activity. Sightings of the strange phenomenon developed into a local folktale that claimed the cloud was carnivorous and would suck the flesh off a person's bones. It was blamed for the disappearance of at least a dozen people, although no one can recall their names. This phenomenon occurred in the area of the last Timucuan stronghold, in the seventeenth century. One folk story suggests a connection between the pink cloud and an Indian legend about Chief Tomokie, who violated local religious practices by seizing a golden cup and drinking from a sacred spring that was said to have healing powers. (Was this the Fountain of Youth?) Anyway, this offense caused the surrounding tribes to attack his tribe. Chief Tomokie was unhurt in the battle, but a beautiful Indian maiden named Oleeta drew her bow on the great chief and put an arrow into his heart. She rushed forward and grabbed the golden cup from the chief's hand, only to be struck down herself with a poisoned arrow. She was still clutching the sacred cup when she died. Legend has it that the cup is still in the possession of Florida Indians. Allegedly, Chief Tomokie's spirit was compelled to wander forever in the mists of the Tomoka River. We don't know if the pink cloud has anything to do with this legend, but an unusual monument topped with a figure of Chief Tomokie can be seen at Tomoka State Park in Ormond Beach.

Only Their Bones Were Found

I remember two things from growing up in Samsula just south of Tomoka Farms Road. We used to go out that road at night to see the Tomoka light. We'd go at night and sit there for a while watching, and then here it would come down the road. It was a glowing red ball of white light. There were also stories of a pink cloud in the woods that would eat the meat off human bodies. Several people disappeared in the woods, and only their bones were found. I don't know how true that is, but I recall seeing the Tomoka light many times as a teenager in the sixties.—*Bob*

It Would Eat the Flesh Off Your Bones

There's a lawyer I know that could fill you in more on the pink cloud. What it was nobody knows, except it was like a thick pink fog that covered a wide area of the Tomoka forest. Now there are claims that many people vanished in that area and only their bones were found. The pink cloud was blamed for the disappearances, and people said it would actually eat the flesh off your bones.—*NSB*

No One Knows What It Was

The only thing I can tell you about the Tomoka pink cloud is that it would devour your body if you got too close to it. It was not always there, but many deer hunters came upon it during deer season. No one knows what it was. Some said it was swamp gas, and some said it was old Chief Tomokie protecting his happy hunting grounds. I don't think anyone has seen it since about 1965. That whole area is now built up with new homes.—*Jimbo*

It's Just Fog

They called it the cannibal cloud when I was in school, and it was supposed to be pink and would eat the meat off anybody that came in contact with it. It wasn't swamp gas; it was more like a fog that really didn't cover but a small area in a low spot. If you go into the woods called the Tiger Bay preserve right near the Tomoka River, you might be able to see it. I don't think there is anything to the cannibal stuff or people disappearing. I think it is just fog that reflects a pinkish color in that area. Most of these newcomers who have moved in don't know anything about it; you have to talk with people who were around in the sixties to hear about it.—*welder2*

Pink or Orange?

The pink cloud was actually more orange-ish in color. It was like a heavy fog and was supposed to be poisonous to breathe and that may be the reason people vanished in there. They may have died from breathing it, and then their skeletons would be found later by somebody. In that same area was the Tomoka light that we used to go see when I was in high school. I saw the light once, and it moved toward my car like my car was drawing it like a magnet. I believe it was swamp gas, but I don't have an answer for that cloud.—*Buck*

Unexplained Booming Sounds

Over the past fifty years, Floridians have periodically heard unexplained booming sounds. These acoustical mysteries have occurred in both the atmosphere and underground. In the 1950s, booming sounds were frequently heard in the Ocala National Forest, but most of those were attributed to the military's Ocala Bombing Range. However, in more recent times, similar sounds have been heard over a wider area without any apparent connection to military activities. People say the noise is like a supersonic aircraft breaking the sound barrier. Windows rattle and the ground shakes, which leads some to believe that the sounds were coming from underground.

On January 25 and 26, 1994, several sonic booms were heard across central Florida, with reports coming from Leesburg, Ocala, Gainesville, Dunnellon, and as far east as Deland. Seismographs at the University of Florida, which are capable of detecting vibrations as far away as China, showed no record of the acoustical phenomenon. When contacted by the authorities, local military installations at Tampa and Jacksonville said the sounds were not made by military aircraft. Likewise, the Federal Aviation Administration could offer no explanations for the bizarre booms. A few people claimed to have heard a quick double boom, similar to what central Floridians experience when the space shuttle breaks into the atmosphere just before landing. However, there were no shuttles flying during this period.

All of these cases continue to baffle scientists. In February 1969, people on Jacksonville Beach reported hearing strange rattling sounds coming from two overhead clouds. A woman described the sound in a newspaper article as being "like constant crumpling of cellophane." There were no abnormal weather conditions that day, no storms or any other possible cause for the rattling clouds. Just one week later, the same unexplained phenomenon was experienced by Miami Beach residents.

In November 1985, unexplained booms were heard at the Kennedy Space Center following a shuttle launch. The mysterious sounds had nothing to do with the launch. NASA clammed up about it, but researchers later found that the same thing had happened after the two previous launches. One physicist theorized that the booms could have been caused by the Soviets testing a secret electromagnetic weapons grid system, which allegedly focused on the space shuttle in order to make technical adjustments in a worldwide electromagnetic grid network. The theory was, at the least, intriguing.

Felt the Earth Move Under Her Feet

I am sure you heard about the strange booms that were heard in central Florida. We heard them in Pine Hills too, and I thought it was the shuttle coming in, but it wasn't. Everyone was talking about it being a small earthquake, but it wasn't. We were outside, and what I heard was two back-to-back loud muffled booms, and with each one you could definitely feel the ground shake. Does anyone know what caused this?—*Patty K.*

Sound Came from All Around

A long time ago when we lived just outside of Fort White, Fla., there was a loud sound that sounded like an artillery gun. This was a rural area, and everybody was pretty much aware of things and knew that nobody was dynamiting anything. We were puzzled by the sound, but what was more odd is that nobody could agree on which direction the sound came from. Some said it was in the air, and others said it was from the ground, and some said it was east or west or north. It was like it was all around. I think that was in 1962 or '3, but the recent booms that were heard in Brevard County reminded me of what we heard. I'd bet it was the same thing that caused it.—*Mrs. J.W.K.*

The Oviedo Lights

On the road between Chuluota and Snow Hill, at the bridge crossing the Econlockhatchee River, there is a ghost light that some claim has been known to chase cars. This phenomenon has been seen for at least fifty years and is called the "Oviedo," or "Chuluota," Lights. Since the 1950s, high school kids from all over the county have driven out to the bridge over the Econ just to check out the lights. They are not always there and seem to favor the warm months. This is one phenomenon that *Weird Florida* has seen and that, to us, looked like a very faint glowing ball of fog rising up from the swamp. Usually there is only a single ball of light, but on rare occasions, as many as five have been observed at the same time. Some witnesses have reported lights that look like the headlights of a car or lights that come down the road and then just stop and hang in midair.

Some people think that the Oviedo Lights are caused by swamp gas. If not for their strange behavior, the swamp-gas theory would seem likely, since the lights are seen mainly in the warmer months, when vegetation decomposes and releases bio-gases. These gases can ignite under certain conditions to produce a glowing effect that rises with the warm air. With all the new development in the area, the lights are now being seen by a brand-new audience, and people suspect that something other than decaying biomass is causing the strange phenomenon.

A Historian's Recollection

The Oviedo Lights were as famous in the late '60s and early '70s as Spook Hill was to us teenagers. You had to go sit on the side of the road and wait till the wee hours of the morning. Usually it didn't happen until after midnight. There were always two lights, about 3 to 4 feet off the ground, and they were light green-colored. They would come zooming around the curve in the road, just like car lights. Occasionally the two lights would hover in the woods too. I remember a write-up in the newspaper saying it was swamp gas or reflections of real car lights that were way, way down the road and that, due to swamp gas and fog, the lights were reflecting nearly a mile away. Whatever it was, it was fun for a bunch of us teenagers who wanted to scare the daylights out of each other.
–*Christine Kinlaw-Best, central Florida historian*

That's My Story, and I'm Sticking with It!

The Oviedo Lights have always been an attraction for young people, especially in the 1960s, when kids would come from Orlando and Winter Park in long lines of cars right through the center of downtown Oviedo. Usually the first car would stop and ask local boys at the Pure Oil Station, "Hey, you know where the Oviedo Lights are?" They would then be given directions to Snow Hill Road and the bridge out there. Then the boys at the station would just roll with laughter and sometimes even help the tale along. Kids would drive to the bridge late at night, turn off their lights, and sit and wait. Sometimes they had their dates, who would get scared at every little cricket or frog chirp and scream, "What was that?" They were all city kids.

Some nights would be very clear, and other nights it would be very foggy and the fog would roll down the Econ and make a sort of swamp-gas effect, which would give off an eerie sight, and with the phosphate in the water, it would reflect any kind of light, including moonlight, car lights, flashlight, etc. Back then any armadillo traveling through the palmettos sounded like a bear, and red reflection in raccoon and deer eyes in the darkness all made for interesting sights and sounds. And if you've ever heard two coons fighting in the middle of the night, it sounds like somebody is getting killed. Local young men would help the Oviedo Lights episodes along by making catcalls, owl hoots, or flashes from lights worn on their heads.

But then the Oviedo Lights caused a terrible accident to happen—this is true. Two boys, who will remain unnamed, were out there driving with their lights off, and one killed the other one with the car. Both were from Oviedo High School. It was a terrible accident, and after that, the Oviedo Lights died down for a long time and started back up again in the 1970s & '80s, and has been going on strong ever since. For those of us in the know, we feel sad when the lights are brought up and try to play them down at Halloween. That's my story, and I'm sticking with it.—*Karen Jacobs, Oviedo-Chuluota historian*

River Runs Backward

There was a boy killed at that bridge across the Econ, and at the moment when you see the lights, the river starts running backward. Most people are always watching the lights, so they don't notice the river, but it will switch course and run backward. Then when the lights are gone, the river starts running forward again. Now try to explain that.—*Sam*

Multiple Globes of Light

The Chuluota Lights have been seen for as long as I can remember. Sometimes it is only a single light, and other times there will be multiple globes of light that drift up from just below the bridge. I have seen this on two occasions, and both times the lights looked like very faint greenish balls of glowing fire. Some people have said it is swamp gas, but I don't know. All that I can say is that it is something that has been seen there for many years. It is strange that it is only seen at the particular spot.—*John T.*

It's Not Swamp Gas

I learned about the Oviedo Lights last night [May 2004]. I heard three different stories about experiences from the same person. They were sitting under the bridge about this time two years ago, and over the top of the bridge, you could see the silhouette of someone looking down and over. Two of the people ran to the top of the bridge on different ends, and there was nothing there. It happened again a little while later. Another time, a bunch of them were sitting on the bridge waiting and

waiting and finally just gave up. They parked their vehicles, and 2 of them walked off about 20 yards. They heard a faint scream and running. The scream got louder and closer. They ran over to the rest of the group, and everybody quieted down, and now the sound of a woman screaming and running footsteps were really close. They jumped in the cars and left. One time out there, they actually saw the lights pull right up and behind them. So the story of it only being swamp gas, I believe, is false.—*Anonymous*

Aerial Phenomena

Like so many other states, Florida has had its share of UFO sightings. Since the peninsula sticks out like a sore thumb, perhaps it makes a good target for space travelers, or perhaps they want to check out the Kennedy Space Center.

Gulf Breeze in Florida's panhandle has been one of America's hotbeds of UFO activity ever since a man named Ed Walters took some photographs of a strange craft there. Everybody flocked to Gulf Breeze for nightly UFO watches, and Ed published a book. UFO enthusiasts still go there, but some say the best place is Mosquito Lagoon on Florida's Atlantic coast, which is within the federal land-management area of the Kennedy Space Center.

Since the late '50s, there have been numerous UFO sightings in this area, usually preceding a missile launch. One of the earliest occurred at night in 1967, when a couple of commercial fishermen from nearby Oak Hill observed a "glowing flying saucer moving slowly over the water." They said it was a greenish object that made a soft whirring noise. When it got too close for comfort, the fishermen decided it was time to leave the area. The strange object trailed slowly behind them for about a mile before veering off toward the east, where it vanished over the Atlantic Ocean.

One of Florida's best UFO sightings happened one evening in August 1952, when a scoutmaster in Belle Glade was driving a group of Boy Scouts home. Along the way, he noticed what looked like some lights in the woods. He pulled to the side of the road and told the boys to stay put while he checked out the lights. Armed with a machete and a flashlight, the scoutmaster went into the woods. The boys became worried after some time had passed and their scoutmaster had not returned. A deputy sheriff came along, and as the boys were explaining the situation, the scoutmaster stumbled out of the woods looking dazed and scared. He related how he had come upon a clearing in the woods, where he saw a disk-shaped metallic craft hovering just above the ground. He said the object shot a stream of hot spray at him that rendered him unconscious. When he came to, the craft was gone.

This case was investigated by Air Force Captain Edward Ruppelt, who was the head of Project Bluebook, then the official investigative agency for aerial phenomena. The investigation found that the grass and treetops in the clearing had been scorched by heat. An examination of the scoutmaster showed that his hat and arms had also suffered burns.

In March 1965, a hunter was deep in the Everglades when he came upon a cone-shaped craft. Thinking it was the earthly thing to do, the hunter waved a friendly greeting as he approached. However, the craft was not too friendly—the man was knocked down by an intense beam of light that allegedly rendered him unconscious for twenty-four hours.

Unidentified flying objects of just about every shape and size have been seen at one time or another in every county in Florida. The oldest account we could find was recorded in the 1871 journal of Josiah Wilcox, who wrote, "Coming down by Cedar Key we seen a big fire come down at night and sit on the shore of the island. We watched it [illegible] over the shallows for some length of time, I would say ten minutes or better, then it shot like a gun straight up

to the sky." That might make Mr. Wilcox Florida's first witness on record of a UFO.

In more recent years, reports of aerial phenomena in Florida have centered on sightings of a strange triangular craft. Between 1992 and 2004, there was a rash of flying-triangle sightings, with dozens of reports made to UFO organizations and an equal number to Internet sites dealing with anomalies. Witnesses also said they saw objects shaped like wedges, arrowheads, boomerangs, and even flying wings. Have space aliens relegated their old flying saucers to the galactic antique-vehicle museum and now travel in a newer model of spacecraft? Or could witnesses be observing a secret experimental craft of our own government? Whatever is the case, don't expect any solutions to this weirdness from either the space aliens or the government.

Fort Myers Triangle, August 1998

I was wondering if anyone saw several flying triangle UFOs in Southwest Florida between midnight and two o'clock on the morning of August 24, 1998. We observed a large triangle-shaped craft flying over west Fort Myers that appeared to be glowing on the bottom side, and it was moving extremely slowly from the south to the north like it was following the Gulf coast. I know there must have been other people to see this thing, because it was very visible. It made no noise and was about the altitude of a small aircraft, but it was not a plane.—*Anonymous*

(note: Several reports of this object were made to UFO organizations and local authorities during July and August 1998.)

Air Force Sergeant Sees Triangle Near Pensacola, October 1999

We were at Fort Pickens State Park fishing when we saw a very odd airborne object approaching from the Gulf of Mexico. I've been in the air force for ten years in aviation maintenance, and I have no idea what this thing was. It was shaped like a triangle and moved at a rapid rate on an erratic course. It first approached the coast at an estimated 1,000–2,000 feet altitude before reversing its heading westward over the Gulf. Several times it just stopped in midair hovering like a chopper—but it wasn't a chopper. This was at night on 9 Oct. '99 between 2000 and 2100 hrs.

What was strange was it was lit by a strange bluish light that seemed to be arching around the object like static electricity or St. Elmo's fire, which is sometimes experienced on aircraft. At times, this glow appeared more yellowish or orange but would go back to bluish again. I noted an aircraft flying to the east of our location, and I'm sure it must have seen this thing. At one point, the craft appeared to be headed toward the Pensacola navy base; then it went through this zigzag routine and veered westward again. Don't ask me what it was. I'm not prone to seeing UFOs, but if I was, I would say this must have been one. I know one thing—it was no military aircraft.
—*Tom K. Sgt., U.S.A.F.*

Boomerang Over Deltona, January 18, 2004

I live in Deltona, between Orlando and Daytona, and would like to mention an unusual aircraft that I saw. I was walking my dog near the golf course at midday, this was not at night, and I had stopped to talk with a friend. The golf course is fairly open, so you can see the sky very well. We saw this object that was shaped like a boomerang; it was very long in length, I must say, at least as long as a football field. Anyway, it came right over us. It was glowing white, so I could not tell if it was metallic. We turned to follow it with our eyes, and the object just disappeared; it like faded out of sight. I think we saw a UFO.—*Mrs. K.B.*

Triangle Seen by Fort Lauderdale Bathers

On May 8, 2004, we were on the beach at Fort Lauderdale and saw a flying craft shaped like a black triangle flying over the Atlantic Ocean. There was a trail behind this craft of rounded smoke rings but not like the contrail behind an airliner. Several people on the beach saw this craft. It was way up there, at least 20 or 30 thousand feet. We guessed it to be at minimum ten sizes larger than the biggest jetliner. We watched it for a minute or two, then it went into a cloudbank and did not come out again.—*Anonymous*

Boomerang Object Sighted Near Space Center

I work at the space center and was on my way to work one morning in 1994 when I noticed a strange object in the sky about as high as a low-flying airplane. At first, I thought it was a plane, but then I watched it and got a very good look at what looked like a real big boomerang or flying wing with three lights on the underside. It appeared to have a metallic skin, very shiny aluminum color. I don't know if it made any sound, because I was in my truck, but it did not put out any exhaust that I could see. I would say that it came in from the ocean and sort of gained altitude once it got over land. It came right over the space center, so I know they must have known about it, but I never could find anybody else that saw it. I didn't want to say too much about seeing it, because somebody might think I've gone looney.—*Joe*

Longwood's Toad Invasion

Residents of Longwood, just north of Orlando, will never forget waking up on May 25, 1982, and finding that millions of toads had invaded their neighborhood overnight. One resident speaking to a TV reporter described the scene as "tons of toads that apparently came from nowhere." Another resident said, "No one is ever going to believe it. This was something that you would have to see for yourself."

Although the toad invasion was confined to only a few neighborhoods, driving in the streets was a nightmare, as cars could not help but squash the poor creatures. They were everywhere. Some people took to swinging brooms at the critters, but they just kept coming. One woman complained on the evening news that the toads had found their way into her house and seemed to be multiplying, while others were diving into her pool like lemmings into the sea.

The mysterious invasion lasted for four days. The streets soon became a nasty mess, with thousands of smashed toads. Residents were out with shovels clearing toads from their driveways and patios. Swimming-pool owners were fishing drowned toads from their pools.

Then all of a sudden, overnight, the toads vanished as quickly as they had appeared. The neighborhood was happy but mystified. Some thought the critters had crawled out of the earth and simply went back into the ground. Others said they had dropped out of the sky. Florida biologists were called in to try to figure out the answer to the toad invasion. They succeeded in explaining at least part of the mystery by identifying the creatures as spadefoot toads, a species indigenous to Florida. The scientists explained how the unusually rainy winter had provided the toads with more water in which to breed. It is a phenomenon that has occurred periodically for a million years, and it could happen again, warned the experts. However, they too were a little mystified at the extremely high numbers of toads; that part is still unexplained. Longwood has not been plagued by a toad invasion since, but as one longtime native remarked, "They should just be glad it wasn't an invasion of alligators."

The Sunshine State's Weird Sky Falls

It is estimated that a thousand tons of matter fall to earth each day. Fortunately, most of it is only in particles. The stuff falling that qualifies as weird includes such things as a green glob, frogs, fish, golf balls, and, of course, a Florida alligator. An alligator did fall out of the sky on May 11, 1911, and landed in somebody's backyard—not in Florida but in Evansville, Indiana! In case you are wondering, the poor airborne gator was killed on impact.

We've had no more falling gators since then, but on May 19, 1959, a frozen chicken egg fell out of the clear blue and almost hit a man in Orlando. One explanation was that a high-flying hen might have laid it while in flight. Experts said that since the egg was frozen, it would have had to have come from an extremely high altitude, and they suggested that it fell out of an aircraft.

But what about golf balls that rain down from heaven? In Punta Gorda, over a hundred golf balls came out of the sky on September 3, 1969. Two possibilities for this one: A tornado picked up the balls from a golf course, or else there were some heavy-hitting golfers nearby.

In August 1970, sunbathers on Playalinda Beach, east of Titusville, reported that thousands of starfish fell out of the sky. The blame was placed on a waterspout, a small tornado over water that vacuumed up the starfish and deposited them on the beach. Good explanation, except no one recalled seeing a waterspout.

In New Port Richey in September 1971, thousands of small fish fell over a wide area and made quite a mess. Experts speculated that fish eggs had been pulled up into the atmosphere and had been suspended in clouds until they hatched. But residents said that the sky fish were too big to have been newly hatched. Too bad they didn't have ice to preserve the fish, like the ice cubes that fell on a Lake Worth residence in September 1978. Supposedly, the cubes, not ordinary hail, rained down over a period of three or four days.

Once again explanations were offered, with experts suggesting the ice falls could have come from frozen water on an airplane's wings. They said that water could have frozen on the wings and that when the plane descended to a warmer altitude, it thawed enough to slip off. Fine, but would it have thawed in neat cubes and blocks?

On February 28, 1958, Miami was hit with another weird sky fall, when a strange transparent globe fell in someone's yard. One observer noted that it looked like a honeycomb. The puzzling object seemed to pulsate, as if it was alive. A police officer stuck his finger into it but said he could not feel anything. When he withdrew his finger, it left a hole in the globe.

When the object appeared to be spreading, the homeowner collected some samples and put them in a jar. But after a short time, the stuff dried up. The same happened with the globe—it disappeared. No one could ever explain what the globe was or why it had fallen out of the sky.

There's the Beef!

Florida ranks eleventh among America's top cattle-producing states. With the Sunshine State's livestock industry bringing in $1 billion a year, it's no wonder the Florida Cattlemen's Association became concerned when cows were being mysteriously mutilated. "Hell, I don't care if it was space aliens, devil worship, secret government stuff, or something else," remarked ranch foreman J. D. Metts. "Somebody's got to do something about it. This costs cowmen money."

Florida is not alone in trying to figure out this riddle of the range; the western states have also experienced strange cattle-butchering incidents for years.

The first suspected case of cattle mutilation in Florida may have occurred in 1967 on a prairie at the headwaters of the St. Johns River. *Weird Florida* spoke with the cattleman who owned the cows. When he came upon his dead cows out on his range, he at first thought their demise was due to some hunters with bad eyesight. But then he saw that there were no bullet wounds, and closer inspection showed that the tail, tongue, ears, and one eye were missing from each cow and that there was no blood on the ground. These parts had been carefully removed with what looked like surgical skill. After a few days, the carcasses began decomposing, but vultures and other scavengers seemed reluctant to go near them. The rancher recalled, "It was like those dead cows were poison."

In 1992, a full-grown bull was found near Samsula with its head cut off. The site was well back from the nearest road, and according to one official, "It looked like the bull had been killed elsewhere and dropped there." The head was found nearby without horns or ears. The Volusia County sheriff's range patrol investigated the case and reported that the "bull's head had been neatly cut off and there was no blood or identifying marks [on the animal]."

The big questions are who would be stupid enough to approach a fifteen-hundred-pound bull and cut its head off, how would you lift and transport the heavy body of a bull, and, lastly, for what reason—just to get a couple of ears and horns?

During the fall hunting season of 1994, two hunters came upon five mutilated wild boars in the woods near Osteen. The animals were in a thick palmetto scrub five miles from the nearest road. Each hog was missing its ears, tail, eyes, and a hoof. There was no sign of a human connection, no footprints or tire prints, and not one drop of blood. "It was no hunter that killed them pigs," said Buddy Harrison, who, along with his partner, had found the dead

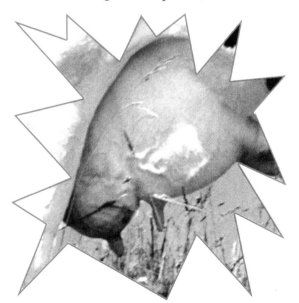

animals. "A hunter would never waste meat like that."

Even stranger is the fact that several hunters who knew about the incident reported that for several nights around midnight, a helicopter had been flying over the area. They thought the chopper had been from the sheriff's department, but a check with the Volusia County sheriff's office found that it was not theirs.

Whether the copter had any connections to the mysterious hog mutilations is pure speculation; however, it is worth consideration, since helicopters have been reported in locations of cattle mutilations in the western states and in Alabama. In the Alabama case, the strange choppers were traced to Fort Campbell, Kentucky, which is the base for the 160th Special Operations Group, the major element of the so-called "Delta Force." We know this sounds like a conspiracy theory getting ready to emerge, but isn't it a little weird for military helicopters to be in the same place—and at the same time—as the cattle mutilations? Military officials, as expected, denied having any aircraft in the area.

Strange mutilations headlined Central Florida news on February 19, 1996, when a dozen cows were found dead in several counties. Law-enforcement agencies in Brevard, St. Lucie, and Indian River counties launched an investigation but could not figure out the bizarre butchering. Some UFO buffs suggested it was space aliens doing the deed. Law enforcement tried to link satanic worshippers to the macabre killings, but no evidence was ever found that connected the deaths to any kind of religious cult.

In March 1997, the state of Florida formed a task force to investigate the mystery, and the Florida Cattlemen's Association put up a $1,000 reward for information leading to the arrest and conviction of the cattle killers. A former FBI agent who had investigated mutilated cattle in

New Mexico came in to conduct his own assessment of the situation and concluded that "natural factors explained the mutilations."

The theory was rejected by most people. One Melbourne rancher pointed out the surgical precision that was used in removing parts of the cows: "Buzzards do not remove the tongue at its base, and buzzards don't remove ears." Some of the animals had every bone in their body broken, as if they were dropped from a high altitude, and a few cowboys reported seeing black helicopters. In one case, a cowboy fired his shotgun at a helicopter that landed in a pasture, and claimed that after that, the mutilations ended.

A best estimate is that fifty cows were mutilated during 1996 and 1997 in eight counties. The reward offered by the Florida Cattlemen's Association has gone unclaimed. Investigators were left mystified, and Florida was left with another unexplained mystery.

Bizarre Beasts

Some really weird creatures live in Florida's forests, swamps, and waters. Our state's subtropical climate is ideal for hosting a wide variety of fauna, including some displaced or yet to be classified critters. While driving through the Merritt Island National Wildlife Refuge early one morning, *Weird Florida* saw a jaguarundi dash across the road. These slender, four-foot-long, short-legged cats are indigenous to Central and South America, and are certainly not native to Florida.

Most out-of-place critters like this one are fugitives from one of Florida's numerous international ports, zoological parks, commercial animal farms, or circus winter quarters. A few have simply migrated in, such as the armadillo, which first showed up here in 1930. When Hurricane Andrew demolished the Miami zoo, several animals escaped. It would be a fair guess that many of them ended up in the Everglades for someone to stumble across and say, "You'll never believe what I saw!"

But what about those weird, unexplainable critters—the Bigfoot creatures, sea serpents, and red-eyed monsters? Well, for starters, about fifty percent are hoaxes. Of course, that still leaves the other fifty percent for which there is no ready-made explanation.

Believe it or not, new animals are discovered all the time. When African tribesmen reported encounters with a fierce-looking ape-man called "Pongo," skeptics labeled it a myth, until 1847, when the first gorilla was captured. Another example of the "unknown" becoming "known" is the big coelacanth fish that was believed to have been extinct for sixty million years, until one was caught in 1938 off the coast of Africa. So keep these examples in mind when reading about encounters with weird beasts in Florida.

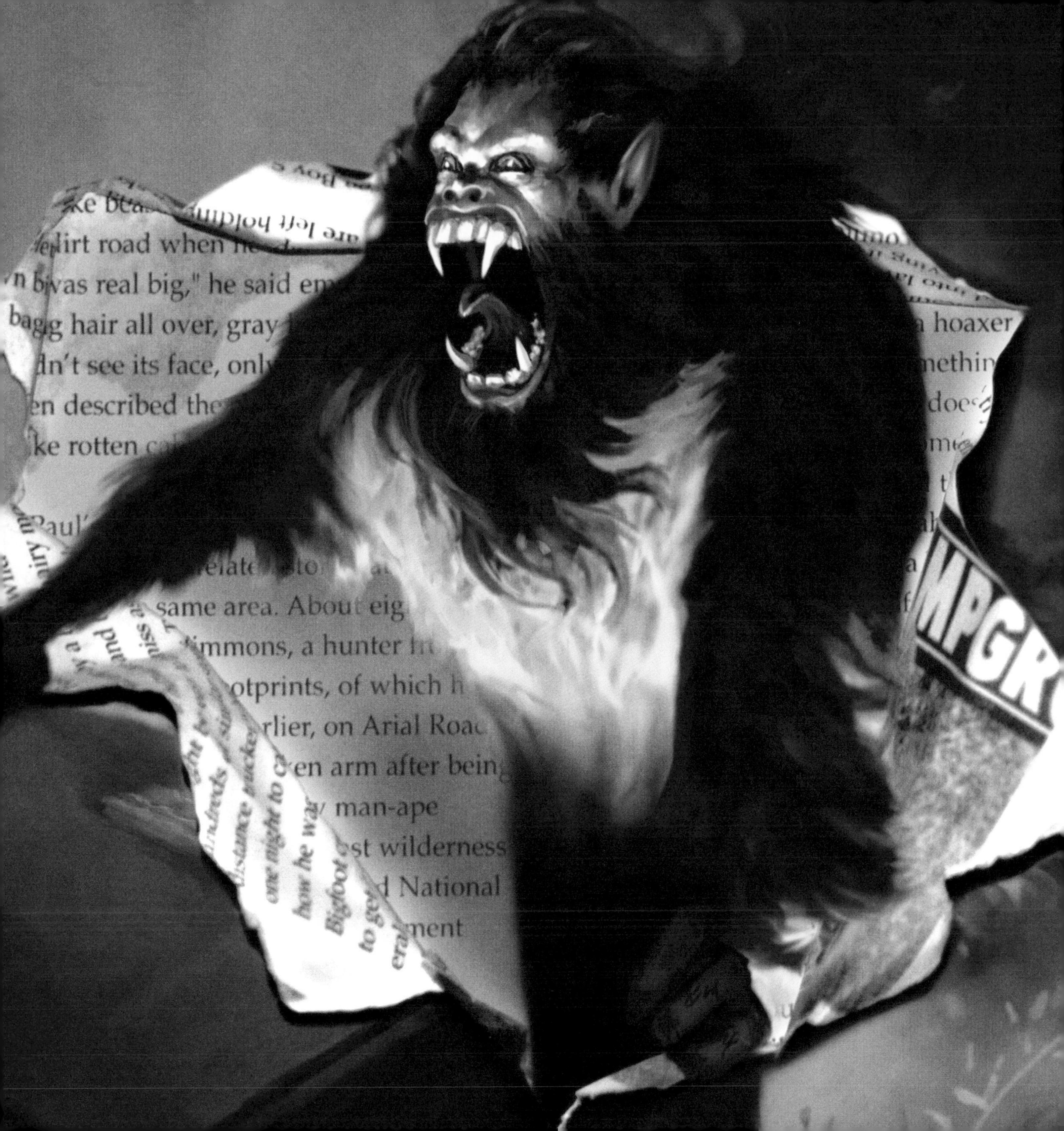

The Mysterious Skunk Ape

If Florida ever selects a mascot to represent all weird things in the state, it would unquestionably be the Skunk Ape. In both size and appearance, this elusive humanoid is Florida's equivalent of Bigfoot. In response to thousands of sightings, the state legislature in April 1977 introduced a bill (H.B. 1664) to protect the elusive man-ape. The bill promised dire results for anyone "taking, possessing, harming or molesting any anthropoid or humanoid animal which is native to Florida, popularly known as the Skunk Ape, or doing any act reasonably capable of harming or molesting such animals." The bill never passed into law, but that hasn't stopped discussions about trying again.

Stories about Skunk Ape encounters may go back to early Indian legends, which tell of giants living along the

Kissimmee River and of the "Sand People" and "Mangrove People." Some believe these legends were describing Skunk Apes. Worthy of consideration is the historical account of Henry Tanner, an early pioneer in Orange County, who told about "finding Indian graves on the St. Johns River with skeletons as big as giants and skulls that would fit over a normal man's head." In 1935, while excavating shells from an Indian mound, workers unearthed "a human thigh bone that was as long as a man's whole leg." Were these the skeletal remains of very big humans or of perhaps an unknown bipedal creature? Once again we are left holding the bag filled with strange stories.

In 1959, three Boy Scouts emerged in a panic from the Ocala National Forest with a wild tale of having been routed from their camp by a big, hairy monster. They said it had a human face and the body of an ape. Now, this might be easy to dismiss as a boyish yarn if not for hundreds of similar stories. Take the one about a long-distance trucker who pulled into a rest stop along I-75 one night to catch a few winks. The trucker recounted how he was pulled from the cab of his truck by a hairy Bigfoot creature. "It came right out of the dark and tried to get in the truck." It carried him under one arm for several yards. "My face was pressed into its hair," the man told a reporter. "It smelled awful." The trucker was able to kick himself free and make it back to his truck. The ape creature began pounding on the truck, but after the driver gave a few blasts of his air horn, it ran off into the woods.

In almost all Skunk Ape encounters, witnesses describe an obnoxious odor, a stench similar to that of rotten cabbage or a skunk. It's this skunklike stink that gives the Skunk Ape its name, although old-timers in rural areas often refer to it as "swamp monkey." One theory is that when it is upset, it gives off a musky odor. It's not just a slight scent either; witnesses have described it as being extremely putrid and strong, enough to discourage anyone from getting too close.

In a 1997 filmed interview, Paul Schmitt of New Smyrna described his encounter with a swamp ape. Paul was delivering newspapers in the rural community of Oak Hill one morning before sunrise when he encountered a "big humanlike beast." He was turning his pickup truck around on a dirt road when he saw the creature in his headlights. "It was real big," he said emphatically. "The thing had long hair all over. I couldn't see its face, only the middle part of its body." Paul then described the classic odor. "There was a terrible smell, like rotten cabbage, so bad that I almost gagged."

What makes Paul's story more interesting is that there are three separate and unrelated stories about Skunk Ape sightings in the same area. About eight miles to the south of this area, Jack Simmons, a hunter from Melbourne, found several large footprints, of which he later made plaster casts. A decade earlier, on Arial Road north of Oak Hill, a girl suffered a broken arm after being thrown from her horse when a large hairy man-ape crossed her path. This part of Florida is a vast wilderness that stretches westward from the Merritt Island National Wildlife Refuge to the St. Johns Wildlife Management Area. With the exception of the highways that cut through this area, a large animal could easily move around here without being seen by humans—well, at least most humans.

Perhaps the best Skunk Ape report was the one made in February 1971 by five archaeologists excavating an Indian mound deep in the Big Cypress Swamp, one of the most isolated areas of Florida. This report involved multiple witnesses and presumably credible scholars. The five men told of an unwelcome beast that crashed into their camp in the middle of the night and wrecked it before running off into the swamp. The intruder was

described as a large bipedal primate without a neck; it was seven to eight feet tall and about seven hundred pounds and was covered with shaggy white fur. The men later found footprints that measured eighteen inches long and eleven inches wide. Typical of other encounters, the witnesses complained about a sickening odor that lingered long after the creature had departed.

In January 1974, the Hialeah Gardens Police Department responded with a helicopter search along a section of U.S. Highway 27 after a motorist reported to the Florida Highway Patrol that he had hit a seven-foot-tall hairy creature that was crossing the road. The shaken motorist said that after he struck it, the beast attacked his car and made threatening growling sounds before limping off into the swamp. At first the story seemed unbelievable, but then two or three other people reported they had seen the creature limping along the highway. One of the police officers involved in the search spotted the big hairy creature about five miles from where the motorist had struck it. While the incident was reported in several newspapers and personnel from both law-enforcement agencies recall the incident, there are no official records of the event, since no formal charges were filed against anyone.

Hard physical evidence of the Skunk Ape is lacking, other than a few questionable plaster casts of footprints. Some hair samples were submitted for analysis, and in 2000, a few photographs were taken of an alleged Skunk Ape in Collier County. There were no scientific conclusions from the hair samples, and the photographs have been disputed by experts as probable hoaxes.

Skeptics have asked, "Where are the bones? Surely Skunk Apes must die and leave behind skeletal remains." The answer is simple: We know that deer and bears exist in the woods, but try to find a deer or bear skeleton. Bones simply do not last long in Florida's subtropical environment.

If there is a conclusion to the Skunk Ape enigma, it would be that credible people, often professional people, have seen something that appeared to be a giant two-legged shaggy creature that stinks to high heaven. As a local swamp tour guide who saw one remarked, "I've been out in the woods all my life, and I've never seen anything like it." What these witnesses have really seen remains a mystery. However, if you are outside at night and the crickets stop chirping and you begin gagging on a foul odor . . . go grab your camera, because you might be about to encounter Florida's Skunk Ape.

BROWN SHAGGY HAIR

THREE SKETCHES BY WITNESSES OF A BIGFOOT CREATURE SEEN IN THE OCALA NATIONAL FOREST IN JUNE 1967.

The Bardin Booger

Bardin, a small community on County Road 209A, just northeast of Palatka, has separated its Skunk Ape from all the rest by calling it the "Bardin Booger." You can get the scoop at Bud's Grocery, which writers and curious tourists use as the Booger information center. You can buy a Booger T-shirt there too. There's even a song about the monster, called "The Bardin Booger," or depending on who's singing, is it the "Bardin Boogie"?

The Bardin sightings began in the early '70s, but the first witness didn't file a report until sometime later. The sheriff's department sent out a search party to look for the hairy ape but found nothing. Several locals, especially some of the younger generation, claim to have seen the Booger, usually at a local lovers' lane. Others have blamed the creature for stealing clothes from their clotheslines, and one person reported seeing it carrying a lantern through the woods. The Booger has not been seen in the immediate vicinity of Bardin since the early '80s. However, there have been recent sightings not far away, around Camp Blanding, the Florida National Guard military reservation. Maybe those Bardin folks attracted too many tourists and the Booger decided to move his territory down the road a piece.

Encounter in the Ocala National Forest

My uncle saw something that looked like a Bigfoot about twenty years ago crossing a sand road in the Ocala National Forest. He said it looked like it had a thick, stringy, hairy coat on and it was about seven feet tall but was like bent over when it scurried across the road. There was another man that saw it too. My uncle called it a gorilla, but when he read something in a newspaper about people seeing the thing they call the swamp ape, he said that is what he must have seen. *–Jimmie C.*

Almost Had Collision with a Skunk Ape

I live in Port St. Lucie. A year and a half ago, I was driving on Rt. 70 heading west towards Okeechobee. I was on the outskirts of St. Lucie County when I nearly ran into what looked like a bear. It literally made me hit my brakes real quick, causing me to peel out on the pavement. I backed up and shined a flashlight in the direction that the thing ran to. I noticed a big gap in the foliage to the side of the road. I was convinced it was a bear but then realized that it couldn't have been, because this thing walked upright with its arms to its sides. I was a little freaked out, having nearly died from fright, so I continued on to Okeechobee. The next day, my cousin and I were driving back to Port St. Lucie, and we pulled over and looked at the area where I nearly ran over the thing. We discovered large footprints in the mud. I ran to the car and got a tape measure from my toolbox and measured the footprints from the farthest point on the front to the back-heel region, and it measured 15 inches. From side to side it measured 8 inches. We counted 11 footprints that were widely spaced out. We even measured how many inches it was from one print to another, and it measured 4 feet in between each print. We attracted quite an audience, because cars kept stopping and people getting out. The prints walked along the roadside ditch and faded into a grassy field. I was convinced that I could pick up the trail again because there was an orange grove on the other side of the field. We gave up the plan because we were told to leave by St. Lucie County deputies. I'm convinced I witnessed the legendary Skunk Ape.*–Anonymous*

C. Wilkins

Grandmother Encounters a Suspected Skunk Ape

Here's my story. About twenty years ago in Citrus Park (just north of Tampa), my grandmother owned about a half acre of land that backed up to a fairly large section of woods. One night she was sitting in her home when she heard the dogs barking and raising all kinds of commotion in the backyard. She realized that they were not acting normal and took off outside to see what was wrong. On this half acre, my grandmother lived up front in her home, and my sis put a trailer towards the back. As she made her way around my sister's trailer, she spotted the dogs. She said they were trying to run away from the fence that backed up to the woods. They were tied up. When she came the rest of the way around, she held up her flashlight and aimed it at the woods. She couldn't see anything, but the smell hit her like a ton of bricks. She said it made her gag. The next thing she did was to go to the fence, and when she did, this thing took off. She said you could hear it running through the brush for a good ways. The next morning she went in back of the trailer, this time with my sis and bro-in-law, and they all said you could see where something HUGE had been and the path it left. My grandmother was not a person that could be frightened; but that did put the fear in her. After that night she did not go back in those woods again.–*Anonymous in Lutz*

Swamp Monkey

About three years ago I was driving across South Florida on the Tamiami Trail at about the edge of dark. I saw something that looked like a very tall ape standing beside the highway. Two other cars saw this thing too. We all pulled off to the side of the road and discussed what we had seen. When we stopped, the thing ran off into the swamp. I have no idea what it was, and neither did the other motorists. Personally, I think we saw what people call a Swamp Ape. I really did see it.–*Ham C.*

Locals Call It "Old Harry"

I believe there is really a Skunk Ape or Florida Bigfoot, because about three years ago we saw one drinking from a creek in some woods near Dunnellon. It looked like a gorilla or orangutan but much taller, with a humanlike head and face. I'm not joking, I seriously saw this thing with three other people. One was an elementary school teacher. It was about 300 yards from us, so we were very close, but when it sensed that we were near, it stood up and looked at us for about thirty seconds, then kinda loped off into some tall bushes. We told a man that hunts in the area, and he laughed and said that thing has been around here for years. He was not shocked at all; he just thought it was normal. He called it Old Harry and said that all the local natives know about it.–*Scotty*

Fairvilla Gorilla

There used to be one of these ape things back in 1968 that would show up around the Fairvilla Shopping Center in Orlando when I went to Edgewater High School. This was an urban area and not rural at all, which makes it even stranger. Everybody nicknamed it the Fairvilla Gorilla. The *Sentinel* even called it that in an article.–*Marie*

Taylor Wild Man

There's an infamous man-creature of Baker County called the Taylor Wild Man. He has a body of a man and the head of a deer, huge antlers and all. He lives out in the woods all around North Florida, probably living off raw fish.–*Darla*

Skunk Ape Suspected of Ripping Apart Farm Animals

On the morning of October 17, I went out to feed the chickens and found a horse that had been ripped open at the neck and a calf which had its head torn off. Later I found a paw print about eight inches long with at least three toes. We called the police, but there was no mention at the time of anything like a skunk ape. As word spread of the incident, we got to thinking that two days earlier while sitting in the living room watching TV, there was a rank smell, like rotten eggs. It was so bad that we closed the windows. Patrolman Simboli, who investigated the allegations, drew no specific conclusions, although he did unofficially acknowledge the possibility of the skunk ape, contending that he had seen such a creature previously.

–*Davie, Fl.*

EL Chupacabra Retires to South Florida

This bizarre creature is an import to Florida in the past decade. The chupacabra actually made its debut on the world's weird list in 1975, after a series of farm-animal killings in Puerto Rico. Rural villagers came forth with claims that an unidentified creature was killing their animals in the early-morning hours by biting their necks. It left strange puncturelike wounds on its victims that were inconsistent with any known species. People reported hearing screeching noises and flapping sounds as if made by the wings of a large bird. Eyewitnesses who claimed they had actually seen the creature generally described it as about three or four feet tall, gray in color, with an oversized head, big oval eyes, and a mouth full of teeth. Another characteristic common in chupacabra reports is the sulfuric smell emitted by the creature. Some descriptions offered by witnesses implied the beast was a gargoyle-like being or a Tasmanian devil with webbed wings.

The rash of unexplained killings was first centered around Orocovis, in the mountainous interior of Puerto Rico, where the mutilated remains of sheep, cows, goats, dogs, chickens, and other animals were found almost daily over a period of two months. According to one account, two hundred cows were killed by the mysterious entity. In accounts of goat killings, many people claimed the creature had literally "sucked the insides out of its victims through the eye sockets," leaving only carcasses of skin and bones. Since the bizarre beast lacked a name, locals dubbed it "the goat sucker," or, as translated in Spanish, *el chupacabra.*

Several prominent and credible citizens of Canóvanas came forward with sightings of an entity that "stood five feet high, with powerful hind legs like a kangaroo, big slanted eyes, and a ridge of fins or spines running down its back." One man claimed to have chased the creature, catching it briefly, long enough to look in its mouth and see long fangs before it broke free and disappeared. Chupacabra reports became so frequent that authorities could no longer ignore them. Police organized search parties to look for whatever was killing so many animals. Canóvanas's mayor, for lack of any other explanation, eventually blamed the animal deaths on feral dogs, though rumors began circulating that chupacabras were some kind of mutation resulting from a secret government experiment. By 1996, chupacabra tales had spread throughout Latin America and among Florida's large Hispanic population.

The first suggested chupacabra report found by *Weird Florida* appeared in a 1996 newspaper article concerning sightings in Sweetwater. (There are four Sweetwaters in the state. This one is a community of mostly Hispanics, located on Route 41 west of downtown Miami.) The report was made on March 10, when a woman said that an "inhuman thing" had crossed her property. This was followed by two more reports, about a strange animal killing two goats and twenty-seven chickens. That was enough to start the ball rolling.

On July 23, 1996, the evening news on most Florida television stations carried a story about a strange beast that was killing people's pets in South Florida and leaving behind a sulfuric smell. Although the C-word was never mentioned, rumors began circulating in Hispanic neighborhoods that this was indeed the work of a chupacabra.

In Tampa, two men reported that a chupacabra had killed some chickens, and claimed to have seen the creature on two different nights. We are left with three possible explanations for the appearance of these strange bloodthirsty creatures in Florida: The first is that they were imported from the Caribbean, perhaps on a cargo ship; the second is that it is mere folklore; and the third is that the infamous Jersey Devil has retired to South Florida. But before making any judgments, read what others have said about Florida's chupacabra.

Definitely a Chupacabra

I would side with the belief the animal mutilations in the Miami area were definitely caused by a chupacabra. When one is finally captured, I don't think it will be all that astonishing and will just be viewed as a new species. They have been seeing these animals for many years in the islands, and I think one somehow came on a ship and got loose. If you check, you will see that all the sightings have been near the Everglades, which is like the climate in the islands, and these animals would have no problem surviving. I looked at the map, and it appeared to me that all the sightings were right on the edge of the glades.—*c7869*

Chicken Takeout for Chupacabra

My grandparents live in Sweetwater. My grandfather had a coop that he kept chickens in. One night he heard noise around the coop, and the chickens were going crazy. He got up and went to look with a flashlight. The coop is a

THE DAILY EXAM

'CHUPACABRA ATTACK FARME IN CHILE!

large square frame covered with chicken wire and is partly covered on top with a flat roof. When my grandfather shined his flashlight, he saw something sitting on the roof that looked like a small kangaroo with big eyes that reflected red in the light. Whatever it was jumped off the coop and hopped away real fast. My grandfather said it really went fast, as fast as a dog can run. He then checked the coop, and out of eight hens, six were dead. One was lying outside, and the rest were inside. There was blood and feathers all over. Whatever it was tore the wire open, and that takes a lot of strength, so it wasn't anything like a possum or raccoon. This was in February 1997. I think it was the same thing people call the chupacabra. I asked my grandfather, but he had never heard of a chupacabra. His neighbors are Spanish, and when we told them what happened and I said something about a chupacabra, they agreed and said it could have been one.–*Chuck W.*

Her Boyfriend Saw One

My boyfriend is from Puerto Rico, and he told me about seeing one of these things when he was nine years old. He is 37 now and is well educated. He said that it looks like a kangaroo with horns and dorsal fins and has long claws. He said that he believes that one of these things was possibly shipped either on purpose as a pet or by accident to Miami and it escaped.–*Alena*

Chupacabra Cover-up

The U.S. government does not want us to know about these creatures, because they are part of an ongoing genetic experiment and if somebody captured or killed one, it would blow their cover. All you have to do is look at where they have been seen. In Puerto Rico, they have been seen around that big telescope that belongs to the government. In Florida, all the sightings have been around the missile bases in Dade and Monroe counties and in Hillsborough County, near Eglin AFB. Now what does that tell you?–*DZ*

Florida's Water Monsters

An old newspaper article dating from 1891 tells of a sea serpent on Jacksonville Beach. The news item stated that bathers ran for high ground when an ugly long-necked serpent reared its head out of the surf. The creature was described as having "a long skinny neck and a dog-like head." That sounds a little like Scotland's famous Loch Ness monster.

That article sent *Weird Florida* in a search of other odd sea-serpent reports in old Florida newspapers. Surprisingly, there were several independent articles related to water monsters in Florida. In 1885, a ship moored in the New River inlet found that its anchor had snagged on something. When the crew finally brought the heavy anchor up, they saw that it had hooked a dead serpentlike carcass. The creature was described as being over forty feet long and six feet wide, with two front flippers and a long skinny neck. It was in a bad state of decomposition and was never scientifically studied, but it would sure smell like a dead plesiosaur to a cryptozoologist.

Octopus Giganticus!

On November 30, 1896, a gigantic mound of flesh from a marine creature washed up on the beach at St. Augustine. The weird, bulbous-shaped, rotting blob weighed five tons and was twenty-three feet long and eighteen feet wide. Dr. DeWitt Webb, a local physician and amateur natural scientist, examined the mass and at first thought it was the remains of a whale. But there was no skeletal structure, and there appeared to be several tentacles. His conclusion was that it had to be a supersized octopus. But the biggest octopus on record was a mere one hundred twenty-five pounds. Webb took several photographs and prepared specimen samples, which were sent to leading marine biologists. Professor A. E. Verrill, a cephalopod expert at Yale University, eventually identified the huge creature as a new type of giant octopus. He wrote a paper on the species, describing it as having tentacles reaching seventy-five feet and a girth of twenty-five feet. The species has since been referred to as *Octopus giganteus Verrill.* Before decomposition, the one that had washed ashore at St. Augustine probably measured a hundred to two hundred feet from the tip of one tentacle to the other. It was indeed a real sea monster.

Octopus giganteus Verrill 1896

The Sea Serpent with the Human Face

When the late Emily L. Bell of Fort Pierce wrote her memoirs about living in Florida between 1875 and 1890, she told of her encounter with a sea serpent. The Bell family went by boat to Jupiter Inlet and, after landing there, struck out on an eight-mile walk along the coast to their destination. Mrs. Bell recalled that along the way, she heard something in the bushes and motioned to her husband, who then investigated. She wrote that it was "a sea serpent of some description. It was green and black with a yellowish mingled color and we watched it crawl into the sea. It raised its head and looked all around till it turned and a human-like face could be seen. It stood up about three or four feet." She added that it was about thirty feet long and the width of a "nail keg." When they mentioned their sighting to other people, they were told the creature was seen about twice a year and that the "Indians, being superstitious, would not kill or capture it." In 1927, another one of these creatures was seen, which prompted some Fort Pierce men to grab their guns and go after it, but by the time they got to the location, the serpent was gone. Is it a folk story, or did these people encounter one of Florida's water monsters?

Modern Monsters of the Deep

We don't have to look in the historical records to find accounts of water monsters in Florida. Some of the best sightings have occurred in relatively recent times. In 1943, a couple sailing off Fort Walton Beach encountered a strange animal with its long neck protruding four to five feet out of the water. Described as having a round head with a furry, catlike face, the animal circled the cou-ple's boat and vanished beneath the water.

In the mid-1950s, there was a series of water-monster sightings in the St. Johns River from Lake Monroe up to Lake George. Dubbed the "St. Johns River monster" in the local newspapers, the creature was said to look like some kind of prehistoric animal. Most sightings were by boaters, who saw the creature submerged in the river with only its head sticking out of the water. Many witnesses claimed to have observed the animal munching on water hyacinths along the riverbank. One man said he saw the strange animal completely out of the water, grazing on grass. He stated that "it looked like a brontosaurus but not nearly as large." In a separate report, another observer claimed to have seen a "path made by the monster in the bushes along the river; the grass and everything was mashed-down where this thing had been eating."

In most accounts, the St. Johns River monster fits the description of a manatee, which can grow to fifteen feet in length and weigh fifteen hundred pounds. Manatees graze on vegetation and have gray elephantlike skin and huge paddlelike flippers. It is reasonable to suppose that they accounted for at least some of the sightings, but certainly these animals don't have furry catlike faces and don't leap out of the water to munch on grass. In some accounts, though, the St. Johns River monster is described as being pinkish and resembling a dinosaur called a thescelosaurus, which lived sixty-five million years ago. The only problem is that this dinosaur was a plant eater that lived on land. Still, a lot can happen in sixty-five million years.

In 1975, there was a sighting of a different type of monster in the St. Johns River at Jacksonville. A group of pleasure boaters said they were startled by a creature that looked like a dragon. It was described as having a "horned head like a big snail." Could this have been the same sea serpent that had chased bathers from the surf on Jacksonville Beach back in 1891?

The most bizarre, and certainly the most vicious, sea-serpent story to hit the press was in 1962, involving five scuba divers off Pensacola. The men were diving from a small motorboat in the Gulf of Mexico within sight of land when there were indications of an approaching storm. They decided to head for shore, but they never made it. As they prepared to leave, they heard tremendous splashing in the water, as if something was headed for their boat. They were startled when a creature that looked like a telephone pole topped with a head suddenly rose out of the water. It was some kind of sea animal with a ten-foot-long rigid neck, a head with tiny eyes, and a wide-open mouth full of teeth. The creature began whipping and thrashing in the water and then dove under the boat. In one account, the craft overturned, spilling the men into the water; in another, the men jumped overboard when it seemed the monster was going to attack the boat. The five men became separated in the choppy sea as the creature whirled and splashed among them.

According to the newspaper account, the testimony given to the authorities came from the only survivor of the ordeal. The assumption is that the others were fatally attacked by the creature or they drowned.

There could be several known-animal explanations for the sightings of monsters in Florida's waters. Take the oarfish, for example; it grows up to twenty-five feet in length and has a snakelike body. How about a school of dolphins with their undulating humps protruding just above the surface of the water? Would that not look like a single sea serpent? Another possibility is a giant sturgeon. Although very rare since 1900, according to the Florida Fish and Wildlife Conservation Commission, one did wash up in March 2002 at Shore Acres on Florida's

Gulf coast. (That one had ten pounds of eggs inside—a whole bunch of caviar!) Then there is the basking shark, whose carcass could easily be mistaken for a rotting plesiosaur. Someday perhaps we'll know for sure what these witnesses really saw. Certainly it was something weird. In the meantime, they've left us with another Florida mystery to ponder.

Unidentified Sea Creature Observed While Deep-Sea Fishing

In October 2003, we were deep-sea fishing about twelve miles out from Canaveral and saw a big ocean creature of some kind. This animal appeared to have a series of large fins down its back side, like zigzags or sawteeth. It was very dark in color. We guessed that whatever it was must have been about thirty feet long. We did not see a head, just the back. It was swimming like a snake would swim, not up and down like a dolphin. To me it looked like a very huge anaconda with zigzag fins down its back. We watched it for several minutes at a distance of fifty yards, then it went under, and we didn't see it anymore. I have no idea what it was but thought you would like to hear about it.—J.M.R.

Convinced It Was a Sea Monster in the River

First let me say that I am a true Floridian and have lived here all my life. I have been in almost every body of water in the central Florida area. Here's my story: On Father's Day of 2002, I had gone fishing with my boyfriend and his parents on the land that runs along the St. Johns River. Our location was right off of SR46, before Moss Park Road's entrance. It was a nice day, so the fish weren't biting. Getting bored, I took my pole out of the water and was relaxing and chitchatting with my boyfriend's parents. Whenever I am near a body of water, my eyes are always glued to it, so staring out at the river, I saw something unexpected come up. I have no idea what it is that I saw. I know this was not a manatee. I have seen manatees a thousand times. This thing was coming out of the water similar to how a porpoise comes up for air. But it didn't have a dorsal fin. The part that was out of the water was about 7–8 feet in length, was at least 3 feet in circumference, and had a shape like a big snake. Its color was dark gray, like a whale, but I didn't see the head and I didn't see a tail either. When I saw it, I said, "What the heck is that?" and I got up to get closer to the water. When it went back in the water, it created some wake with a little white water. I have never seen anything like this before, especially in the St. Johns. I know it was not an alligator. I am convinced that I saw a sea monster. The thing never resurfaced in the area that we were in. What confuses me even more is that the area of the river that we were in is pretty much a high-traffic area. If anyone knows anyone that has seen this or could have an explanation to what I saw, I would love to hear from them.—*T.H.*

Remembering the St. Johns River Monster

I remember the Johns River monster from when I was a kid. For a couple of years, there was a lot of hoopla about it in the paper. I still have an article from the *Sentinel Star* about a man near the mouth of the Oklawaha seeing one crawl out on the bank and start eating the vegetation. I never saw it, but my uncle was a commercial fisherman in Lake George, and he saw something that looked like a head on a long neck come out of the water and look around and go back under. He said whatever it was looked like it had a dog's head. I think he said the neck part was about 12 feet long. Nobody believed him, but he swore that he really saw it.—*Shorty*

The Case of the Giant Penguin

Numerous people reported seeing a giant penguin on Clearwater Beach in 1948. The huge bird was said to be fifteen feet tall and supposedly left big tracks along the beach. During this same period, people in a boat off the Gulf coast reported seeing an extremely large penguinlike bird floating on the water. These incidents were written up in several newspapers. That same year, another big penguinlike bird was seen by a private-airplane pilot on the banks of the Suwannee River in northern Florida. The famed investigator of the unknown, the late Ivan Sanderson, conducted a scientific inquiry into these sightings. No conclusion was ever reached or any explanation provided.

Local Heroes
and Villains

Every place has its unusual characters, both living and dead. This chapter features a few select people whose deeds, good or bad, set them apart from ordinary folks. Some of the people you'll read about here contributed to society in a strange way. Others robbed the local bank and shot the sheriff. Whether they come from the backwoods or from royalty, their stories are equally curious.

You may find these folks to be mysterious, eccentric, magical, or downright mean and disgusting. But whatever they are, they have added color to the fabric of Florida's cultural background.

Searching for Lewis Powell's Head (and the Rest of Him)

In the Geneva community cemetery, beneath the shade of a half-dozen old cypress trees, is a rather peculiar grave containing only a skull. It's all that remains of Lewis Thornton Powell. Whether he was a villain or a hero largely depends on which side of the Mason-Dixon Line you're on. Lewis Powell, you see, was a Florida Confederate soldier and a conspirator in the assassination of Abraham Lincoln. So, you may wonder, why is only his head buried in a little cemetery northeast of Orlando?

Lewis Powell was the youngest son of Reverend George and Caroline Patience Powell's eight children. The family had lived in Alabama and Georgia before settling in Live Oak, Florida. At the outbreak of the Civil War, the seventeen-year-old Lewis enlisted in the 2nd Florida Infantry in Jasper. Two of his brothers, George and Oliver, also served in the Confederate army. George was killed in the Battle of Murfreesboro in Tennessee, and Oliver returned home crippled.

Lewis suffered a wound to his wrist at Gettysburg, where he was captured by Union troops and sent to a prison hospital in Baltimore. In September 1863, two weeks after arriving at the hospital, he escaped and made his way to Virginia, where he joined Mosby's Rangers of the 43rd Virginia Cavalry Battalion. The records indicate that Lewis Powell's service with the Virginia cavalry was "distinctive." However, in January 1865, he deserted and crossed to the Union side. Using an alias — Lewis Paine — he took the Oath of Allegiance to the Union.

There is strong speculation among historians that Powell switched sides and changed his name because he was a secret Confederate agent. It is known that he became involved with John Wilkes Booth in a scheme to kidnap Abraham Lincoln. The plan was to trade Lincoln for Confederate prisoners of war, but when the mission did not work as planned, Booth hatched his infamous plot to assassinate the president and other high-level Union officials. Lewis Powell was recruited for this mission, along with David Herold, George Atzerodt, and Mary Surratt.

Each conspirator had a specific role in the mission. Booth was to shoot the president at the same time that Powell was to kill Secretary of State William Seward. In order for Powell to do his part, he had to go to the home of Seward, who was recuperating in bed from a carriage accident.

On the evening of April 14, 1865, Booth shot Lincoln at Ford's Theatre. But Lewis and David Herold ran into unexpected difficulty at the Seward home. Four people were stabbed inside the house before Lewis could make his way up to Seward's bedroom. He stabbed the bedridden secretary of state several times and then in a panic ran from the house. Seward survived the attack but was left disfigured for life.

After evading the authorities for three days, Lewis showed up disguised as a laborer at the home of co-conspirator Mary Surratt. Unfortunately for him, he arrived at the very time Surratt was being arrested, and he was taken into custody as well.

At his trial, Lewis sat like a statue while his attorney, W. E. Doster, argued his innocence by claiming, "He lives in that land of imagination where it seems to him legions of southern soldiers wait to crown him as their chief commander." Instead of a coronation, though, Lewis and his fellow conspirators were hanged on July 7, 1865, in the courtyard of the Old Arsenal Building in Washington. In 1869, all the bodies were claimed by relatives for reburial except the body of Lewis Powell, which remained in a lone grave.

Meanwhile, back in Florida, the Powell family, fearing retaliation after a Jacksonville newspaper exposed them as relatives of a Lincoln assassination conspirator, moved from Live Oak to the rural seclusion of what is now Oviedo, then in Orange County.

Lewis Powell's body was reburied at least once in the Washington, D.C., area, but later his remains mysteriously became lost. In 1992, his skull, identified by museum catalogue numbers, was discovered among American Indian skeletal remains in the Smithsonian's Museum of Natural History. No one knows what became of the rest of him or how his head ended up with Indian bones at the Smithsonian. Perhaps the rest of his skeleton is still stored in a dark corner of some Washington warehouse.

The Smithsonian located his closest living relative, Helen Alderman of Geneva, Florida, and released the skull to her. Using her own funds, she arranged a proper interment. On November 12, 1994, in a Confederate memorial service, a small mahogany box containing Lewis Thornton Powell's skull was buried next to his mother's grave in the Old Geneva Cemetery.

The Wizard of Central Florida

There is a small frame house on Sixth Street in Sanford that looks like an ordinary house unless you know the inside secret. This is the domain of Wise the Wizard, a magician who can change a live rabbit into a dog or pull a city-block-long string of silk scarves from an empty box. Now if that doesn't qualify as a wizard, then we don't know what does. But please don't ask for the secret of how it's done, or you might feel the wrath of the wizard's wand. The wand belongs to Harry Wise, a magician who once entertained thousands on theater stages across America and Canada.

The Great Harry Wise is more than just a magician; he is also America's last ghost-master. What's a ghostmaster, you ask? Well, first you'll need to know about the old ghost shows. These were live horror shows that were presented from the 1920s through the 1960s on movie-theater stages, usually in conjunction with midnight shows that featured a scary movie. They always opened with a little bit of magic and featured various illusions, pseudohypnotic acts, a cast of monsters roaming through the audience, and, in the middle of the show, a total blackout of the theater, leaving the audience squealing in the dark. Producers of these fright fests were called "ghostmasters."

Among the most famous ghost shows was Doctor Jekyl's Weird Show, and the

infamous Doctor Jekyl was none other than the Great Harry Wise, often referred to as the "master of horror." Wise played his last live ghost shows in the 1970s in Daytona and New Smyrna Beach, making him the last in the nation to produce a true ghost show in the old style. When movie theaters began eliminating stages, ghost shows and other live stage acts faded into showbiz history.

Harry Wise began his entertainment career at age eighteen, when he put on a magic show for the local grammar school, for which he was paid $25. The next night, he was on the stage of Sanford's historic Ritz Theater. "That was Halloween night," recalled Wise. "I actually launched my stage career on Halloween night." His big break came when he joined the famous Johnny Cates's ghost show out of Houston, Texas. In this show, Wise played the Frankenstein monster on stages all across the country.

In 1959, Wise formed his Doctor Jekyl's Weird Show, based in Florida, and took it on the road, spreading his ghoulish mayhem up the West Coast, through the midwestern states, Canada, and down the eastern seaboard to almost every movie house in Florida. The show featured two blackouts of the theater, throwing snakes into the audience—that's rubber ones—and Doctor Jekyl always managed to "chop off" a fan's head with his infamous guillotine. Old newspaper articles have referred to his show as "the show with 1001 horrors, so scary that you'll have nightmares for a week." This kind of press was just the ticket for a show. During the 1970s, Wise performed in both nightclubs and theaters under varied monikers: Darkveil, Dark Vale, Mr. Magic, Doctor Jekyl, and Wise the Wizard. He shed all those titles in 1980 to become Hans Voglar, "world famous mentalist." He toured college campuses and clubs, mesmerizing fans who, recounts Wise, "really thought I could read their minds. It was a real study in like being a stage magician." But after a year of "reading minds," Hans Voglar became Harry Wise again.

Wise went beyond being a showman *extraordinaire*; he is also a dedicated humanitarian. While he is quick to boast about the years he spent in entertainment, he seldom mentions his contributions to good causes. He once raised enough money to get operations for twenty-two crippled kids at the Harry-Anna Crippled Children's Home. His efforts also purchased the first tanker truck for the Forest City Volunteer Fire Department. When a volunteer fire department in Orange City needed a Jaws of Life, Wise put on a show that raised enough money to buy one. And when financial troubles were about to close a home for wayward girls in Brevard County, he raised funds through his magic to save the home. Maybe this is the stuff that separates real wizards from everyday magicians.

In 1982, Wise did something that he had wanted to do since he was ten years old—he joined the circus. "It was my lifelong fantasy!" exclaimed Wise. "I just had to get it out of my system." And so he did. During the 1980s, he toured as a ringmaster for a total of four different circuses before returning to the stage with his big two-hour magic show.

Harry Wise admits that "most of my illusions are trick," but note the word "most." Does that mean that some of them are real magic? His response is, "Not actually magic, as you think. There's a lot we don't understand about the physics of the universe, and some secrets are best left alone for now." That would sound like a magician trying to create a little mystery if not for what we learned from one of Wise's former stage men.

The rumor is that the Great Wise has a secret tucked away in three safety-deposit boxes in an undisclosed bank. It is so guarded that the first two boxes each contain a key to a third box in a bank out of state. It would take two people with two different keys to open that box. The secret is supposed to be instructions for something, perhaps a grand magic trick or a secret the great magician has stumbled upon during his travels. Or is it just an ongoing act? Wizards create illusions, after all.

Wise's life in show business is reflected in a permanent exhibit at the City of Sanford Museum. Yet the most amazing thing about Harry is not open to the public. It is his house, which is indeed a wizard's abode, filled with over fifty years' worth of magic and fantasy. Mystery literally permeates the air in this weird dwelling, an archive filled with stage props, talking skulls, top hats, magic wands, and theater posters from hundreds of performances, with hardly enough room to walk or sit. Someone else might see it as a mystical time machine of sorts, guarded by unseen unicorns, where the past and future are rolled into one . . . or maybe the past is really the present . . . or whatever you want it to be. From the outside, this strange dwelling looks like any ordinary house on Sixth Street. Or is that an illusion as well? Remember, this is the house of a wizard.

The Infamous Ashley Gang

The notorious Ashley gang was southeastern Florida's equivalent of Jesse James, Bonnie and Clyde, and Al Capone all rolled into one criminal package. Between 1911 and 1924, these brazen but often bumbling bandits left a trail of crime from the Everglades to Jacksonville. Their reputation was so bad that just about every major crime in South Florida was pinned on them, whether they did it or not.

In the shadows, aiding and abetting the gang's career of crime, was a young woman named Laura Upthegrove. Known as the "Queen of the Everglades," she was a big girl with a tawny complexion. She was said to be always armed with a .38 and would shoot a man at the drop of a hat.

John Ashley and his brothers—Bill, Bob, Ed, and Frank—were raised in a typical cracker family in the tropical backwoods along the Caloosahatchee River near Fort Myers. Their father, Joe Ashley, was a skilled woodsman who made his living by fishing, hunting, and trapping otters. In 1911, the family moved to West Palm Beach. Oddly enough, Joe Ashley, a law-abiding man, served briefly as a deputy sheriff in Palm Beach County. But young John Ashley, who had become an expert trapper and alligator hunter, spent most of his time in the Everglades. It was during this period that young John turned outlaw and earned the title "Swamp Bandit."

On December 29, 1911, a dredging crew near Lake Okeechobee found the body of a Seminole trapper named Desoto Tiger. An investigation revealed that John Ashley and Desoto Tiger had been seen together on their way to market with a boatload of otter hides. Authorities learned from fur dealers that Ashley had sold the hides in Miami for $1,200. John Ashley had launched his criminal career by murdering his Seminole partner for otter hides.

Two deputies caught up with him as he was camped in a palmetto thicket near Hobe Sound. They moved in to make the arrest but instead found themselves looking into the barrels of pistols held by John and his brother Bob. The Ashley brothers

disarmed the deputies and told them to warn the sheriff "not to send anymore chicken-hearted men with rifles or they are apt to get hurt." The Ashleys were said to fear no lawman. (Yet as ruthless as they were, the gang always stuck to one gallant rule—they never robbed women.)

John Ashley fled to New Orleans. But by 1914, he was back in Florida, hiding out in the Everglades, where he was joined by one or two of his brothers and any other desperado who wanted to get in on the action.

In 1915, John, with the help of his brother Bob and a Chicago mobster named Kid Lowe, attempted to rob a Florida East Coast passenger train. The robbery was less than successful, though, because the gang hadn't worked out who was to shake down the passengers and who was to rob the mail car. They had more hard luck later that year, when they pulled off a daring raid on a bank in Stuart for $45,000 in silver and currency. During this heist, Kid Lowe accidentally shot John Ashley in the jaw and destroyed his right eye. When John tried to get medical attention for his eye, he was captured and locked up in the Dade County jail to await trial.

SHERIFF
ROBERT BAKER

THE NOTORIOUS ASHLEY GANG

JOHN
ASHLEY

RAY
LYNN

MOBLEY
HANFORD

THE KING
AND QUEEN
OF THE
EVERGLADES

ROY "YOUNG"
MATTHEWS

CLARENCE
MIDDLETON

On June 2, 1915, Bob tried to bust his brother out of jail. Not one to beat around the bush, Bob went to the jailer's house, shot him at point-blank range, and took the jail keys. He then ran from the house to a garage where his cronies had stashed a getaway car. Unfortunately, Bob couldn't drive the kind of car that had been left for him, so he tried to force several men at gunpoint to do it. The men all claimed not to know how to drive the car either. Bob was in a real fix, so he jumped on the running board of a passing truck and forced the driver to take him out of town. By this time, a deputy was in pursuit of the truck, which stalled in the middle of the street. A shootout erupted, which ended in the death of both Bob and the deputy.

Then Kid Lowe, perhaps trying to atone for shooting his buddy, sent a note to the sheriff's office threatening to shoot up the whole town if John Ashley wasn't released. It was an empty threat. John was found guilty of murder and robbery and on November 23, 1916, was sent to the state penitentiary at Raiford.

But no jail could hold John Ashley for long. He escaped, did a little moonshining, was caught and sent back to jail, then escaped again, this time for good. While John was incarcerated, the gang members had occupied themselves mostly with moonshining, sometimes livening up things by hijacking rumrunners, but with the return of their leader, they went back to the big time: robbing banks.

In November 1924, they robbed a bank in Pompano. After cleaning out the vault and cash drawers, they wrapped the loot in a bedsheet, then drove through the middle of town in a stolen taxi waving a bottle of whiskey, shouting, "We got it all!" They crossed a canal and disappeared into the swamp near Clewiston, pur-

sued by a posse led by Sheriff Fred Baker. The gang was found camped out near a moonshine still. A gun battle ensued, and when the smoke had cleared, Sheriff Baker was dead. John Ashley escaped into the wilderness. A short time later, Laura Upthegrove and some other gang members were arrested, but John remained at large.

The slain Sheriff Baker was replaced by his son, Robert Baker, who vowed to put an end to the Ashley gang once and for all. A tip from an undisclosed inform-

ant, believed to have been the girlfriend of one of the outlaws, told Sheriff Robert Baker that the gang would be driving at night up the coast, heading for a bank they planned to rob in Jacksonville. The sheriff determined that the bridge over Sebastian Inlet, about twenty-eight miles north of Fort Pierce, would be a perfect spot for an ambush. But the location was out of Baker's jurisdiction, so he asked the sheriff of Indian River County to handle the operation. Baker sent three of his deputies to assist in carrying out the plan.

The lawmen blocked the road at Sebastian Inlet by

stretching a chain with a red lantern across the narrow wooden bridge. After about an hour of slapping mosquitoes, the deputies saw an oncoming vehicle that fit the description of the gang's big black touring car. Taking up their positions, they waited for the car to stop and then approached it from behind. It was the Ashley gang, all right.

The deputies ordered the gangsters out of the car, then searched them and the car, finding several guns. The deputies thought they had found all the weapons, but while the gangsters were being lined up outside the car, John Ashley pulled out a concealed gun. The deputies immediately opened fire, and when it was over, John and three other gang members were lying dead in the middle of the bridge.

The deceased gangsters were buried just outside Gomez, in the family cemetery in the woods where the old Ashley shack once stood. There are six members of the Ashley gang here, all but one dead from bullet wounds.

Today, the little Ashley cemetery is no longer in the woods. It sits in the middle of an exclusive residential development of multimillion-dollar homes called Mariner Sands. How

TODAY, THE LITTLE ASHLEY CEMETERY IS NO LONGER IN THE WOODS. IT SITS IN THE MIDDLE OF AN EXCLUSIVE RESIDENTIAL DEVELOPMENT OF MULTIMILLION-DOLLAR HOMES CALLED MARINER SANDS. HOW IRONIC THAT THE INFAMOUS MEMBERS OF THE ASHLEY GANG ARE NOW RESTING IN THE MIDST OF MILLIONAIRES, INCLUDING SEVERAL BANKERS.

ironic that the infamous members of the Ashley gang are now resting in the midst of millionaires, including several bankers. There's a rumor that buried somewhere on this property is some loot that was never recovered by the gang.

Laura Upthegrove, the notorious Queen of the Everglades, lived under an alias for a while in western Florida. After several arrests, she ended up running a gas station at Canal Point on Lake Okeechobee and lived with her mother in Upthegrove Beach. Following an argument with a man who accused her of shortchanging him in a purchase of moonshine, Laura grabbed a bottle of disinfectant and drank it. Some said it was an accident, that she thought it was a bottle of gin, but others claimed she committed suicide. Whatever the case, she died within minutes. She was only thirty.

A state historical marker that chronicled the violent end of the Ashley gang once stood at Sebastian Inlet, but it disappeared when a new bridge was built over the waterway. No one knows what became of it. Perhaps it was stolen by some criminal.

Bone Mizell

One of the most colorful characters in Florida's history was a rugged cracker cowboy named Bone Mizell, who loved horses and whiskey. Born Morgan Bonaparte Mizell in the settlement of Horse Creek in 1853, he was the son of one of Manatee County's earliest pioneers, Morgan Mizell. Bone stood a lean six feet tall, spoke with a lisp, and had skin tanned like leather. He grew up in the saddle, working the cattle ranges between Orange County and Okeechobee for big cattle barons, like the Parker brothers and Ziba King.

In those days, Florida cowboys were known as "cracker cowboys," "cow hunters," or "cowmen," and the scrub cows they herded were often called cracker cattle, a scrawny breed that evolved from the early Spanish cattle. According to one source, the word "cracker" is derived from the sound made by the ten-foot-long braided rawhide whips that were snapped or cracked by cowmen during cattle drives.

Bone never learned to read or write, but he had an uncanny ability for remembering hundreds of cattle brands and whom they belonged to. Of course, this was a good skill to have, since he also did more than his share of cattle rustling. But he was also known as a generous man and a legendary prankster, full of humor.

Bone, who said that hard drinking would kill him someday, got so drunk one night that he passed out. A group of fellow cowboys decided to play a trick on him, so they carried him to the cemetery and laid him down between two graves. The men then hid in the graveyard to wait for sunrise. The next morning, Bone woke up, rubbed his bloodshot eyes, looked around, and said, "Here it is Judgment Day, and I'm the first one up!"

There is an unconfirmed tale about the time Bone got revenge on one of Florida's cow towns for some slight forgotten by history. A circus had set up near the railroad tracks, so Bone waited for the big top to fill with people and then tied a rope from the tent to an outbound train. When the train pulled out, so did the circus tent.

In the 1890s, Bone gained a notorious reputation for cattle rustling. He was arrested several times for changing brands on cows and hogs or for branding unmarked livestock. There were rumors that some of his rustling was done for one of the big cattle ranches. In 1896, he was convicted of rustling and sentenced to two years in the state penitentiary.

Bone's loyal friends circulated a petition asking that he be pardoned, but were told he would have to serve some time in prison before that could happen. So wearing a new suit bought by the same friends, Bone boarded a train and headed for prison. When he arrived, the warden gave him the grand tour and invited him to dinner. After eating, Bone said, "Well, now that I've served time, can I have my pardon now?" He was pardoned and boarded a train the next morning for home.

When the artist Frederic Remington visited Florida in 1885 to study the cattlemen, he used Bone Mizell as the model for his well-known painting *A Cracker Cowboy*. Although Bone never realized it, this would be his ticket to everlasting art fame. His likeness appeared in *Harper's Weekly* and in a metropolitan New York newspaper. Remington wrote of Bone and his cohorts in *Harper's Weekly*, "As a rule, they lack dash and are indifferent riders, but they are picturesque in their unkempt, almost unearthly wildness." Remington preferred western cowboys over Florida cowmen, but his painting is an excellent depiction of a Florida cowman of the 1880s.

On July 14, 1921, Bone Mizell went to the Atlantic Coast Line depot in Arcadia, Florida, to send a telegram to the Lykes Brothers meat company in Tampa asking for a loan. Afterward, he lay down on the waiting-room bench. The station agent, Robert Morgan, told Bone to sit up and asked if he was okay. Bone replied, "Yeah, I guess I better sit up because if I lay down I might die." The agent left for lunch, and when he returned, he found Bone sprawled out on the floor. The local doctor was summoned to check him over. Without examining the body, he took one look at Bone and pronounced him dead. A bystander protested, "Why, you didn't even test him to see if he's dead." To which the doctor replied, "Don't need to, that's old Bone Mizell, if I tested him he'd test 90 proof."

Morgan Bonaparte "Bone" Mizell died at the age of sixty-eight and was buried in the Joshua Creek Cemetery, near Arcadia. On his death certificate, the doctor listed the cause of death as "moonshine, went to sleep and didn't wake up."

Count Von Cosel and His Immortal Love

During the Great Depression, Count Carl Von Cosel, a fiftysomething German immigrant, worked as an X-ray technician at the U.S. Marine hospital in Key West. Actually, he was not a count, and his name was not Carl Von Cosel. It was Carl Tanzler, but he did come from Germany, where his ex-wife and two daughters lived. The "count" made many claims—he had nine university degrees, had been a submarine captain, and was an electrical inventor. In truth, he was a lonely man living in a fantasy world.

While working in the Marine hospital, he met a twenty-two-year-old patient named Elena Hoyos. A beautiful Cuban, she had been an entertainer before contracting tuberculosis. Von Cosel fell in love with her even though she consistently resisted his advances. From her X-ray reports, Von Cosel knew that she had only a short time to live. He convinced the young patient that he could cure her with a special X-ray machine, combined with daily doses of a certain tonic made from gold and water.

Von Cosel began administering his "miraculous" treatments to Elena, along with a proposal of marriage. But despite his promises to restore her health, her disease progressed, and she eventually died. She was buried in an ordinary grave, but Von Cosel obtained permission from her family to move her body to a nice stone mausoleum. During the move, he discovered that Elena's body had never been embalmed and was in a horrible state of decay. The bereaved lover hired a local mortician to clean and fix up the body before placing it in the new tomb. What the family did not know was that Von Cosel had the only key to the crypt.

Von Cosel became morbidly obsessed with Elena and secretly visited her in the crypt every night, bringing gifts

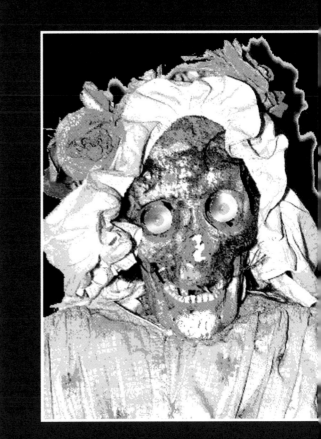

He secretly transported the corpse to his house on Flagler Street. He dressed Elena in a wedding dress and often slept with her as his wife. To keep her body preserved, he rubbed it with various oils, chemicals, and perfumes to mask the odor of decomposition.

and flowers. According to some accounts, he installed a telephone in her tomb so he could talk with her. He believed that she could communicate with him through voice and song.

After two years, Von Cosel removed Elena's remains from her tomb and took them to a makeshift laboratory he had built inside the wingless fuselage of an old airplane behind the Marine hospital. There he began work on her corpse, wiring it together and using wax, plaster

of Paris, and glass eyes to restore her to "life." When he learned that the military planned to move the fuselage, he secretly transported the corpse to his house on Flagler Street. He dressed Elena in a wedding dress and often slept with her as his wife. To keep her body preserved,

he rubbed it with various oils, chemicals, and perfumes to mask the odor of decomposition. He continued restoring her facial features using mortician's wax.

Local folks became suspicious that something strange was going on when Von Cosel kept buying perfume and women's clothing and when a newspaper boy reported that he had seen the count through a window dancing with a big doll. This started Frankenstein-like rumors circulating around town, which quickly led to gossip that Elena's corpse was inside Von Cosel's house.

The girl's family was now up in arms, and Von Cosel reluctantly agreed to allow Elena's sister Nana into his house. When Nana saw the corpse dressed in a wedding gown and propped up in a chair, that was it. She immediately went to the police.

Count Von Cosel was arrested and charged with graverobbing and abusing a corpse, but by the time the case went to trial, the statute of limitations had run out and no sentence was imposed. During the trial, Von Cosel told the court that he had planned to use an airship to take him and Elena "to the stratosphere so radiation could penetrate her tissues and restore her to life." What really outraged the judge was that Von Cosel asked if he could have Elena's body back!

Because there had been so much publicity about the case, officials decided to put Elena's corpse on public display at the local funeral home so the curious could view it. Afterward, the remains were placed into a metal box and buried in a secret location. None of this put an end to Von Cosel's weirdness. He began charging tourists twenty-five cents to tour his laboratory; after the tourists stopped coming, he dynamited Elena's mausoleum and left town. He died in Zephyrhills in 1952, clutching a life-size doll with a face that resembled Elena's. It was later learned that Von Cosel had secretly made a death mask of his former bride of death.

Florida's Invisible World of Magic, Hexes, and Luck

In rural graveyards, people frequently find silver, melted candles, playing cards, dolls, notes, chicken feet, and other weird items placed around tombstones. Authorities investigating such reports usually determine these things to be connected to satanic worship. In some cases, this is true, but often they are evidence of hoodoo practice.

Hoodoo is basically described as southern folk magic and is not the same as voodoo, which is a religious practice. Hoodoo is a belief system that uses roots, herbs, charms, powders, and spiritual energy to bring luck to someone or to cure ailments or to simply put a hex on an enemy. Practitioners of the craft go by many names, like root worker, mojo, juju, conjure doctor, two-headed doctor, and black Gypsy. Two of the most famous hoodoo doctors, long since dead, were Dr. Buzzard of the Carolina low country and Aunt Caroline Dye of Arkansas.

Hoodoo is not as widespread as it once was, but there are still a few rural communities in Florida that have root workers. It is not easy to get an interview with one. In the first place, root workers prefer to deal with a small number of clients, and in the second place, they have a fear of being charged with practicing medicine without a license. After attempting to contact three root doctors, *Weird Florida* finally got to talk with Mama Jones, who lives in Tampa. And that's all we can tell you about her place of residence. Mama Jones will not give her age, since, as she says, "It don't make no difference," but admits to being part Creole, part black, part Indian, and part white. Her father was also a root worker, having learned the art from his mother. Since being taught hoodoo as a young girl, Mama Jones has practiced it in Georgia, Alabama, and Florida, where she now lives. Our conversation with her went like this.

Weird Florida: Tell us about hoodoo, or root work, as you call it. Is it like witchcraft?

Mama Jones: No, no. Root work is more like that man in the drugstore does, but his is store-bought and mine is natural. It ain't witchcraft or anything like that. No, root work is different, and it's old as the hills. Ever since folks been using things out of the woods to cure theirself, there's been root workers, but now I can make luck too or make bad luck or cure most things.

W.F.: Are there very many like you, and do you ever talk to other root doctors?

M.J.: I talks to some. There be two here that I know, and there is one in Plant City, and there used to be one old juju man in Cross City I knowed. I thinks he's dead now, but there be a few around. That Cross City man, he mostly mixed remedies to cure people, he'd cure just 'bout anything.

W.F.: Tell us how a root doctor cures somebody.

M.J.: Well, I can't say about that, unless I knows what's wrong with them; then I mixes a powder or tonic. I use herbs, some minerals and herbs, it all depending on what be wrong with you. You know that Chinese medi-

cine? Root work be a bit like that, but more magic. You see, there's has to be that spirit energy in there. You know what I'm saying?

W.F.: Sure, but how do you get this spirit energy?

M.J.: You conjure it up. You can get it in the cemetery. You take a jar of water and place it on a tombstone, and that water will soak up that energy just like a sponge. That what happens when you put something on a grave. You can take sand from a grave—it's full of that spirit—and put it on a tomato plant, and that plant will grow like crazy. That's how that energy works.

W.F.: So you use cemetery energy to cure things?

M.J.: Oh, more than that. You take that graveyard dirt and mix it with salt and bluestone and put it in a little pile in every corner of your room, and it will keep bad luck away. It stops all that evil.

W.F.: Why does it keep bad luck away?

M.J.: You look at a room. It has four corners, and if you draw a line from each corner, it makes a big X in the room. That why it works.

W.F.: So a big imaginary X is what is protecting the room?

M.J.: That's what I'm saying—just like a crossroad. You know how streets cross? That's where you have to throw bad luck. You just let it suck up in a hen's egg, and you takes that egg down there and throws it in the middle of that crossroad, and there goes that bad luck. I got to do that when I have leftovers from laying a trick on somebody. I got to take that leftovers down there and throw it in that crossroad.

W.F.: What's in those little sacks on the shelf?

M.J.: Them is mojo bags. You put a mixture in there or silver or something—whatever you need and carry that with you—and it can draw good luck or cure you or whatever. Now, it depends on what is in there. You can put a hex in there and throw it under somebody's porch, and they don't know it's there, and it'll jinx their whole house.

W.F.: Okay, how do you jinx somebody?

M.J.: You don't want to mess with that. That's powerful stuff, and it gots to stay with a conjure doctor. I tell you this—if you get the sand out of where somebody's footprint is and puts it in a mojo sack with certain kinds of herbs and puts it under your steps, that person will stay away. Now, if you draws an X on the ground where a person walks and puts some mixture across his path, that bad magic will go up through his feet when he walks on it.

W.F.: Now, you talked about spirit energy. Does that mean you believe in ghosts?

M.J.: Sure. They're all 'round. You wants the good ones, but them others gots to stay away. They be no good.

W.F.: Then how do you keep a ghost away?

M.J.: You takes a little liquor and pours it in a dish and sits it on your porch. Ghosts will lap that liquor up and go away. Or cross two brooms at your door, and them spirits will stay out.

W.F.: What do people want most from your services—good luck, hexes, or curing something that's wrong with them?

M.J.: Oh, most peoples wants luck nowdays. They be coming here wanting a lucky number; they be telling me about their dreams. I still got an old Aunt Sally dream book, but I can hear a person's dream, and that be enough to pick numbers.

W.F.: You mean like the Florida lottery?

M.J.: That's what I'm talking 'bout—Lotto. It used to be Bolita and Cuba when I was a girl. They called it policy numbers 'cause the numbers man would sell it like an insurance policy. You bought a policy—that was so the law wouldn't get you from playing numbers—but now the state runs all that now.

W.F.: Has anyone ever won the Lotto with the numbers you picked for them?

M.J.: Oh, they did, yes, sir.

W.F.: The Lotto? You mean they got all six numbers, like millionaires?

M.J.: No. I mean they won . . . four numbers, three numbers. One got five numbers. Sometimes their dreams ain't right. You got to get it right, and some folks they be yee-hawing about their dreams to me, and they don't know what they dreamed. You hear what I'm saying? You got to get it right for the right numbers.

W.F.: I really thank you for talking with us about what you do. Before we leave, we want you to pick out six numbers for the lottery.

Ending note: Believe it or not, out of the six numbers Mama Jones picked, three of them hit. Was it an easy five bucks using hoodoo? Or was it just luck?

Personalized Properties

Sometimes it seems that the houses in Florida's residential developments all look alike—or almost alike. Sticking one of those pink flamingos in the yard only makes your place different until the neighbor down the street does the same thing. To be really different, you have to do something outrageous, something that will make people say, "Look at that weird place!"

Some folks have gone way beyond the norm with their piece of real estate. What you see in their yards is a loud declaration of their personality. Decorated properties are unlike mere cluttered yards, because they are intentionally designed. They are an artistic expression or a desire to share a fantasy. Or perhaps they are a public statement protesting an injustice. Whatever the case may be, there's always an interesting story surrounding these special properties.

The Da Vinci of Debris

Somewhere in the rural part of Hardee County, between Arcadia and Bradenton, is a real fantasyland where you'd least expect it. It is miles from nowhere, but if you go to the tiny hamlet of Ona on Highway 64, then follow Horse Creek about nine miles south through swamps and cow pastures, you'll find it. Of course if you don't want to get your feet wet, you can take either County Road 663 or 665 south from Highway 64, and you'll soon see a sign directing you to this most unusual place.

Howard Solomon, an internationally known sculptor, has taken to the extreme the old saying "A man's house is his castle." Using what others have thrown out, he has built a twelve-thousand-square-foot castle complete with towers, a moat, and eighty stained-glass windows. The entire castle is shiny silver, because it's covered with thousands of aluminum printing plates discarded by a local newspaper down the road in Wauchula. Howard is truly the Rembrandt of Reclamation, the Da Vinci of Debris.

When he bought the land, it was during the dry season, and he had no idea it would become a swamp in the rainy months. Being a resourceful guy, he built a levee and pumped the water out. Then he built a moat and, after that, a boat, which he called the "Boat in the Moat." This is no rowboat. It's a full-size sixteenth-century Spanish galleon, complete with masts, sails, cannons, rigging,

and decks. It's sitting right there in the moat, although Horse Creek will never be deep enough to float this craft to the ocean and guarding the boat is an alligator, a "lady gator," according to Howard. But this is not one of Howard's creations. It's real.

Originally from Rochester, New York, Howard is skilled in over twenty trades, including welding, carpentry, painting, cabinetmaking, tinsmithing, plumbing, electrical work, and carving. He doesn't mind telling folks that some people call him "How-weird," and you'll see why during a tour of his crazy castle. There are several large galleries inside, all filled with Howard's quirky recycled creations. He's got a small zoo of animals that he has twisted and shaped out of fifty pounds of coat hangers. There's a two-speed unicycle and a motorcycle that he calls "Evil-Corn-Evil," made from an old corn planter. (In addition to being the Da Vinci of Debris, Howard is also the Prince of Puns.) One wall has a large collection of guns—well, guns according to Howard, like the hernia gun, so heavy that you'd ruin yourself if you lifted the sixty-five-pound weapon. Other weird weapons include the square shooter, with a square barrel, and the suicide gun, with its barrel bent back toward the shooter.

You might wonder how Howard can manage his big kingdom of fantasy. It's because this is a family affair, involving daughters, sons, grandchildren, a few friends, and his wife, Peggy, who takes care of the gardens.

Solomon's Castle has been featured on numerous television programs and in publications around the world. Howard's work reaches way beyond Florida and has been shown in both national and international exhibitions. It is one great enjoyable escape from reality, and the best part is that you can visit. You see, Howard kept adding so much stuff to his property that he had no choice but to open it for tours. If you get a chance to visit this whimsical wonderland, be prepared to laugh yourself silly.

The Mafia House

Long before condominiums popped up in southern New Smyrna Beach, a lone house was built on 127 acres of sand dunes overlooking the ocean. This was in 1969, when southern New Smyrna was a remote area. People began wondering why anyone would want to build a house there, and soon the rumor mill got going. The strange house covered six thousand square feet and was like a fortress, with double-paned bulletproof windows, armor-plated doors, ten-inch-thick steel-reinforced concrete walls, and a helicopter landing pad on top. If that was not enough, there were machine-gun mounts on the roof and an underground shooting range. The house sat on pilings and had two electrically operated drawbridges and an elevator that could lift a vehicle.

Locals could take their pick of rumors about the unsociable owner. Some claimed he was a member of the Mafia. Others said that he was the son of a wealthy doctor or that he was a rich oil-company executive. The truth is, no one really knew much about him until April 20, 1970, when he was found dead in the sand dunes and identified as forty-four-year-old John Maeder of Mount Vernon, New York. Newspaper accounts reported that he had been driving a tractor in the dunes when it tipped over on a fifteen-foot slope and his head was crushed. But near his body were a nickel-plated pistol and three spent bullet casings. Inside his house, the authorities discovered several cases of ammunition, some antiaircraft artillery shells, and several guns. An inquest ruled his death to be accidental, but Maeder's strange ending only added to the mystery.

The house has been dubbed the "Mafia House" by locals, who often use it as a landmark when giving directions: "Go past the Mafia House two miles" or "on the beach in front of the Mafia House." Over the past decades, this once remote area has been

DO NOT ENTER TRESPASSERS WILL BE PROSECUTED

built up with new beach houses and high-rise condominiums. It's a little difficult to find the house now, but it is still there, standing between two high-rise buildings. Several previous owners and renters have reported seeing the ghost of Maeder flitting through the house. There is still no solid connection between the house and the Mafia or other nefarious operations. Then again, there wouldn't be, would there?

Built by the Mob

That house they call the Mafia house has always been there. I think it was built by the mafia a long time ago. There was a man killed there. I think he was shot by the mob, but the reason it was built was so they could use boats to bring drugs in from ships at sea. Anyway, that is the story that I heard.—*ducky67*

Built by the CIA

It's not a Mafia house. That place was built by the government during the Cuban Crisis to watch the ocean around Cape Kennedy. It was a spy nest for the CIA; that is why it has all that James Bond stuff, like thick bulletproof glass and secret gun ports and those railings around the edge of the roof. That used to be a helicopter landing place, and there were all kinds of antennas sticking up, because I remember seeing that. There was a whole string of these houses down the coast. You go to Tybee Island in Savannah and there are some, and down in Miami there are some.—*Robert B.*

Built by a Drug Lord or Something

We went by there one night on the beach. We were walking, and it was after dark, kinda late, and there were like these lights on the roof, and when we looked, we saw a man, and he was all in black clothes and had this like gun or weapon, and he was like guarding that place. Later someone told me that there is no one living there and that man we saw isn't real. I mean, he is a ghost of the man who built that place. He was a drug lord or something. It is creepy at night.—*Kayla*

Built by a Rich Man

We always called it the Mafia house, but I don't know that it had anything connected to the Mafia. It was built in the sixties, when all that area was undeveloped. The man who built the house, as I understand, was a rich oil tycoon and in the shipping business. It is true that he really put up a lot of security around there, but that is expected if you are rich, because you can't tell when somebody might want to kidnap you for ransom. I don't think there is anything evil about it. I do know people who say it is haunted, but I don't know about that.—*Adrian*

Dead Wood Comes to Life in Apalachicola

To say that Ed Moberly makes things out of wood would be an understatement. He has carved so much stuff that he's lost count. We're talking about everything from fish puffing on cigars to parrots with shot glasses to a big black wooden dog chained to his gate. Ed's carvings come in all sizes, from the tiniest to big and bigger. Most are sort of cartoonlike, but what really sets them apart is their brilliant colors, like the tropical Florida landscape.

Ed never sells anything, which is why the yard, porch, and every room in his Apalachicola house is filled with sculptures. The tall sea captain in the yellow raincoat that greets folks in front of the house is called Capt'n Walt Shell, so named for one of the neighbors. There's a big wooden alligator out there too, but Ed keeps him chained to a post.

Apalachicola is Florida's oyster-gathering capital, and when Ed retired here, he wanted something to keep him busy, so he began carving. He's entirely self-taught, but pretty soon he had a yardful of great-looking things, and people were bringing him wood to see if he could make something out of it. "I get my ideas from all kinds of things," he explains. "Someone might bring me a toy or one of those little ceramic souvenirs. Or I might find a picture in a book, and I simply magnify it in wood." He doesn't chop down living trees, but if you drop an old cypress log off at his place, he'll transform it into one of his masterpieces.

Some of Ed's carvings are featured in a bar scene in a movie directed by Victor Nunez entitled *Coastlines*, and several of his larger pieces are in parks around town. Ed has had many offers to sell his work but refuses them all. "One fellow came up with a big deal to market my work. He thought we could make a lot of money, but that's not what I carve for."

Nope, Ed Moberly doesn't want more money. He carves for the pure joy of it. Pretty weird, huh?

Forty Years of Protest in One Home

Grover C. Walker of Winter Park has never given up his protest against the government over an injustice done to him more than forty years ago. Walker is a former army and air force intelligence officer who also served as a special agent for the Pentagon, and his twenty-five-year service record was exemplary. In 1962, owing to cutbacks in the number of officers on active duty, he was reduced in rank from captain to staff sergeant. Walker could have retired at that point as a major in the reserves, but he elected to remain in air force intelligence as a sergeant. Everything went well until September 1965, when he was assigned to the secretive 7113th Special Activities Squadron at Rhein-Main, Germany.

Walker soon found reason to suspect that there were corrupt and subversive activities being carried out in the squadron, possibly by his superiors. When he threatened to blow the whistle, he was whisked off for a superficial psychiatric exam that branded him "chronically para-

noid." For twenty-five years, while working in intelligence, he had been sane. Then, in an instant, he was labeled crazy. Soon after, he was forced out of the air force. Documents support Grover Walker's story, but as he says, "Who will believe you when you've been labeled?"

When Walker's story became publicly known, he was called the "American Dreyfus," because his story closely parallels the 1894 case of Alfred Dreyfus, a Jewish lieutenant in the French army who, as a result of a political injustice, was sentenced to Devil's Island. Dreyfus was eventually found innocent and went on to receive France's Legion of Honor. Weirdly, the fates of both Dreyfus and Walker were decided on December 19.

Upon being booted from the air force, Walker returned to the United States with his family, and after much wrangling, he received his air force pension as a major.

In 1966, Walker began his fight to restore his good name. He painted his house, on Tyree Lane, red, white, and blue and put up eight flagpoles, each flying an upside-down flag as a symbol of distress. On the roof, he had a huge billboard that read U.S. DREYFUS. Walker later erected a ninety-one-foot pole with an upside-down flag and published a pamphlet about his plight.

Along the way, several other former intelligence officers have come forward with similar stories. However, when Walker and his wife began attracting too much

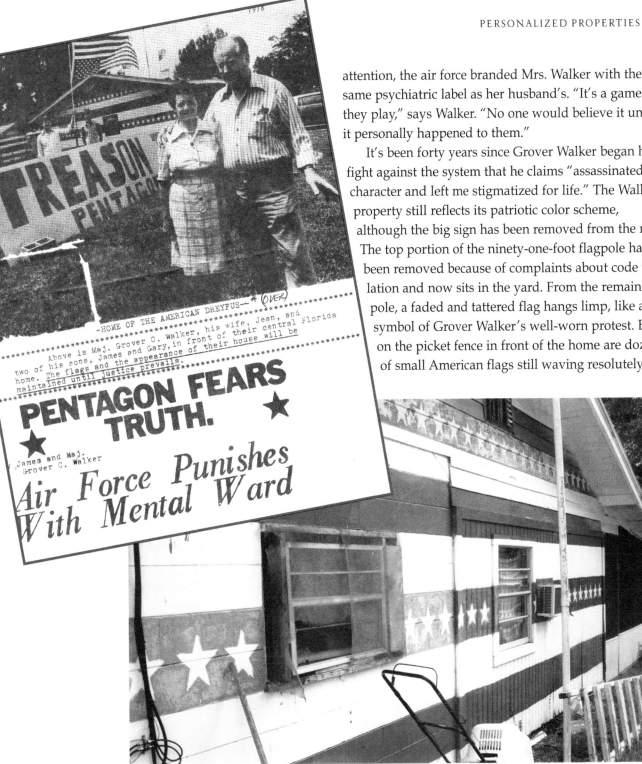

—HOME OF THE AMERICAN DREYFUS—* (OVER)
Above is Maj. Grover C. Walker, his wife, Jean, and two of his sons, James and Gary, in front of their central Florida home. The flags and the appearance of their house will be maintained until justice prevails.

PENTAGON FEARS TRUTH.

James and Maj. Grover C. Walker

Air Force Punishes With Mental Ward

attention, the air force branded Mrs. Walker with the same psychiatric label as her husband's. "It's a game they play," says Walker. "No one would believe it unless it personally happened to them."

It's been forty years since Grover Walker began his fight against the system that he claims "assassinated my character and left me stigmatized for life." The Walker property still reflects its patriotic color scheme, although the big sign has been removed from the roof. The top portion of the ninety-one-foot flagpole has been removed because of complaints about code violation and now sits in the yard. From the remaining pole, a faded and tattered flag hangs limp, like a symbol of Grover Walker's well-worn protest. But on the picket fence in front of the home are dozens of small American flags still waving resolutely.

Grabowski's Gothic Garden

Joe Grabowski's property in Edgewater, Florida, has been magically turned into what he calls a "visual fantasy." People slow down when passing the place just to savor the sight of the unusual landscape, which looks like it came right out of the Middle Ages. "I call it my Gothic medieval garden," explains Joe, who has lived here for the past twenty-seven years. "It has a European flavor and fantasy, with just a touch of country, with a pig here and there."

For the most part, this retired designer for the old Gimbels department store in New York City has taken what others have thrown out and transformed it into art. Joe once hauled broken bricks and blocks from building sites in the neighborhood and then, using spray paint, turned them into ancient-looking rocks and stones. It's an example of how one man's junk ends up being another man's treasure.

"During the Depression, my father worked as a janitor, taking care of an eight-story apartment building, fixing the toilets, furnaces, and things," recalls Joe. "That was back when all the movies were about millionaires, so it was my fantasy to grow up and live like a millionaire. On Sunday mornings, I would gather the pillows around me and have breakfast in bed. I would pretend that my father was the butler; he would bring me a tray of French toast with a flower from the garbage."

Joe sees art in just about everything—bottles, rocks, leaves, broken toys, plastic ornaments, wrought-iron chairs, discarded light fixtures, and a decorated rocking horse that supports his mailbox. "I see beauty in it all," he says. "Flaky, peeling paint or even the mildew look." He also likes sand and dirt, which he rakes in swirling patterns like those seen in Oriental gardens.

Joe has fashioned castles with minarets and fanciful finials from bowling balls, bottles, vases, and golf balls. From across the yard, it all looks like the onion-domed architecture of a miniature Turkish village. In fact, looking at this strange yard, you begin seeing the same fantasies that its creator talks about. It's really a kind of test, because if you don't see a fantasy here, then maybe you don't have much of an imagination. Children have referred to his yard as Harry Potter's place, Alice's Wonderland, and the Ghostbuster place, but to Joe it is simply a labor of love.

"The best compliment I ever got was from a real bully," he says. "I was sitting in my garden, and at a distance, I could hear someone cursing up a storm. The filthy words got louder. I looked down the street and saw two boys coming my way. The cursing got louder, like they were trying to shock the neighborhood. I thought to myself, 'Oh-oh, here comes trouble,' and wondered what they would say when they got in front of my place. Well, all of a sudden the cursing stopped, and so did they, right in front of my house. One of them says, 'I love your place. When I was two years old, my mother would bring me by to see it, and I'm twenty years old now, and I'm still crazy about it.' I said to him, 'You touched my heart. God bless you.'"

Joe's property, or mini estate, as he prefers, is a constantly changing masterpiece. He doesn't mind people coming by to see what he's recently done, unless he's in the process of creating. "I don't like my vision interrupted," he says. "It could take days to get my inspiration back."

Joe may not have those millions that he had fantasized about in his youth, but he has something that money can't buy—an amazingly creative mind and the most unusual yard in town.

THE SEVEN DWARFS' HOUSE

Have you ever wondered where the real seven dwarfs' house is? The one in the story is pure imagination, and the one in the animated film was a drawing. So where is the real one? Believe it or not, it's sitting on Spruce Creek just west of Port Orange, Florida.

In 1898, James N. Gamble bought several acres here, including an orange grove, and built a small cottage and a citrus packinghouse. He called the place "Egwanulti," which is supposedly a Native American word that means "by the water." The property is on the upper reaches of Spruce Creek, which meanders its way east to Ponce de Leon Inlet. You'll recognize the family name. James Gamble was the son of the founder of the Procter & Gamble Company. James was a longtime winter resident and citrus grove owner in Volusia County, but it was his son-in-law, Alfred K. Nippert, who built the dwarfs' house.

When Gamble died in 1932, his property was inherited by his two daughters, Olivia and Maude. Maude was Nippert's wife. Her death in 1937 left Albert looking for something to help him cope with her passing. He became enchanted by the Disney film *Snow White and the Seven Dwarfs* and began planning an exact replica of the dwarfs' house.

In 1938, he hired a carpenter to watch the movie ten times in order to learn every detail of the Black-Forest-style cottage. When it was finished, Nippert's cottage had a fireplace, cypress door handles, stairs to the second level made of split logs, and headboards for the seven dwarfs' beds. Everything was there except the dwarfs. Nippert then surrounded his cottage with a rock garden, a witch's hut, and the dwarfs' mine shaft. The property has always been private and was never open to the public. Walt Disney is supposed to have accepted an invitation in 1939 from Nippert to visit the Gamble home and see the dwarfs' house.

In 1993, the Gamble property was listed on the National Register of Historic Places. As of this writing, it is still closed to the public, but a restoration project is under way that will open the estate to the public in the future, with a public park, a historical and environmental center—and the seven dwarfs' house.

Baghdad in South Florida

This place was originally called Opatishawockalocka, supposedly an ancient Tequesta Indian word meaning "big island in the swamp covered with many trees." Actually, we think it means "word with too many letters that no one can pronounce." In any case, it was too long for a town's name, so developer Glenn H. Curtiss shortened it to Opa-locka. You'll recognize Curtiss as the famous aviation pioneer, who ranks up there with the Wright Brothers, Charles Lindbergh, and Howard Hughes. Curtiss was also a developer in South Florida, who, along with his partner James Bright, purchased 220,000 acres in Dade County. In 1920, when Florida was experiencing a housing boom, Curtiss hired architect Bernhardt Muller to design a town that looked like it was straight out of the Arabian Nights. This was the beginning of the city of Opa-locka, which Curtiss incorporated in 1926 as an "Arabian Fantasy."

The inspiration for the odd development came from the 1924 film *The Thief of Baghdad*, which starred Douglas Fairbanks, Sr. Between 1925 and 1928, Curtiss built 105 structures, including a train station and city hall, both with spiral staircases, onion-shaped domes, minarets, and towers that would have pleased any sheik. The homes, each with its own minaret, were thousand-square-foot bungalows that sold for about $1,300 each in 1927. The streets were laid out with Arabic-sounding names, like Shakar, Ali Baba, Cairo, Harem, and Sharazad, which was shortened from

Scheherazade because no one could pronounce it. When finished, in 1928, this Baghdad of Dade County boasted the largest collection of Moorish architecture in the United States. The only things missing were camels and a desert. When Florida governor John Martin visited in 1927, he was welcomed at the train station by city officials dressed like sheiks and mounted on white horses.

The town was severely damaged in the 1926 hurricane, which destroyed some of the original buildings, but Curtiss kept his project going, building a golf course, a hotel, and a zoological garden. When the Florida land boom ended, he deeded the town to the county.

Opa-locka is well known in military history for its airport, which was previously a base for blimps. This was the place from which Amelia Earhart launched her ill-fated flight around the world. But it is Opa-locka's Moorish-style city hall that attracts the most attention. With its colorful onion-shaped domes, keyhole archways, fountains, towers, and palm-shaded courtyard, it looks like it belongs in Persia. Surely it's the weirdest city hall in America.

Over the years, Opa-locka has suffered from economic decline and social problems, which have left the city's Moorish motif in danger of disappearing. But when the unique city hall was scheduled to be demolished because it had fallen into great disrepair, the townspeople rallied to stop the wrecking ball. That led not only to the saving of the city hall but to a campaign to rescue seventy-two other Moorish-style buildings in the city. In recent years, the community has been hosting an annual Arabian Nights Festival each May that is growing in attendance. The city hall is now listed on the National Register of Historic Places, along with twenty other buildings in Opa-locka.

TIME

The Weekly News-Magazine

Glenn Curtiss on the cover of Time magazine, 1924;
typical Moorish-style home in 1927

The Bowling Ball House

After driving through Clearwater in the bumper-to-bumper rat race of Highway 19, the weary traveler will find a pleasant refuge in Safety Harbor. This is one of those rare places around the Tampa triangle of growth that has retained its charm and friendly nature. No malls and high-rise condominiums here; instead Safety Harbor's main street is home to quaint shops, art galleries, and pleasant eateries—and the bowling ball house on Third Street.

There's hardly an inch of this fairyland property that has not felt the artists' touch.

This colorful fairy-tale cottage is the home and studio of two well-established artists: Todd Ramquist and Kiaralinda. She uses only a single name, the one that appears on her work, which is exhibited around the world. The two artists have spent nearly twenty years creating their folk-art property using mirror fragments, bottles, beads, acrylic plastics, tiles, glass, and five hundred or so bowling balls painted a rainbow of colors. The cottage even has a name, Whimsy.

There's hardly an inch of this fairyland property that has not felt the artists' touch. The yard is lined with bowling balls, some stacked like minarets, others in a large colorful pyramid in the middle of the yard. It's an open-air folk-art gallery, with bottle trees sprouting cobalt-blue bottles, dangling mirrors, and a gaily painted lizard on the wall.

Since old bowling balls have played a big role in Todd Ramquist's art, he and Kiaralinda have produced a photographic book entitled *On the Ball*, featuring eighty bowling balls designed by various artists.

Safety Harbor's bowling ball house has become somewhat of a tourist attraction and is featured as part of the town's annual Holiday Homes Tour. To celebrate the new millennium in 2000, the house was covered in Mylar, and invited guests all wore crazy spectacles. You'll have no problem finding this place—just ask anyone in Safety Harbor. It's the best-known house in town.

Amelia Island's House of Statues

Many people wonder why a home on Amelia Island's Fletcher Avenue has life-size statues standing like gray zombies in the front yard. The answer is easy: The concrete figures are the last of a collection made by Frank M. Klies, great-grandfather of the home's current owner, Ken Huston. The statues have become such an attraction that cars slowing down to look at them have tied up traffic and caused the city fathers to ask Ken to move them. But with each statue weighing over a ton, that's not likely to happen.

Opposite page: Ken Huston poses with statues of the Duke and Duchess of Windsor.

Frank Klies crafted the statues as a hobby, pouring concrete over a frame of shaped-iron rods and metal screen, then etching the final details with a toothbrush and toothpicks. A career navy bandsman, he made the statues in Maryland, where several of them still stand. The statues in Ken's front yard include Abraham Lincoln, Jean Harlow, Eisenhower, and one Marshal Joseph Pilsudski, complete with medals, who was Poland's leader after the First World War. The only statue representing Ken's ancestors is the one of his great-grand-mother, with her arm raised. He said she once held a trumpet, but like all the statues, there has been considerable wear and tear, and some parts are missing.

Not all of the collection is standing on the front lawn. There are three statues in the backyard. One is a reclining nude, which Ken thought was a little risqué to be exhibited on the front lawn. The other two are the Duke and Duchess of Windsor on their wedding day.

Ken is a retired designer and builder of water features, those big elaborate waterfalls and pools that you see at resorts. His work has been featured in *Better Homes and Gardens* and in many other publications. He could probably restore his statues but says it would distract from their historical value. Besides, it's fun to see the poor ol' duke lying there in a garden while his duchess gazes serenely outward.

Roadside
Oddities

Contrary to what many tourists may think, **not all of** Florida's attractions are confined to theme parks. Some of the most unusual are found along the roadsides. No, we don't mean roadkills. We're talking about those wacky man-made things that make us turn our heads as we drive by and say, "What was that?"

Roadside oddities usually lay claim to being the biggest, tallest, smallest, oldest, strangest, or something else we can't figure out. They are Florida's eccentricities to the left and right of the main highways. They sit there, usually in some scrubby place, and beckon us to stop and take a photograph. Given Florida's fast-changing times, tourist photographs may be the only documentation that these things ever existed. Thus we have a duty in the name of weirdness to stop and pay homage to these roadside marvels. And as a bonus, you get to have your picture taken next to something ridiculous.

Zero Milestone

This big six-foot-diameter coquina sphere in St. Augustine sits beside Highway A1A near the visitor center. Perhaps you've seen it and wondered, "What is that big stone ball?" It's the Zero Milestone that was placed here in 1929 to mark the eastern end of the Old Spanish Trail that ran from St. Augustine all the way to the Pacific, where it terminated in San Diego, California. The trail was the first transcontinental route from ocean to ocean.

Big Tree

Longwood's Big Tree, at 3,500 years old, is the oldest living thing in Florida. Think about it: This gentle giant was an adult tree before the birth of Christ. Towering 126 feet, the huge cypress, nicknamed the "Senator," has a girth of 47 feet. Despite hundreds of lightning strikes, it is still alive and well. It was considered the largest cypress in the country until 1970, when a challenger was discovered in a Louisiana swamp, and that initiated a squabble as to who really has the biggest tree. The American Forest Association has now listed the Louisiana tree, located on Cat Island, as the world's largest cypress. The Senator's supporters argue that the Cat Island tree is only 83 feet tall, but Louisiana says it's fatter, with a girth of 56 feet, and has an 85-foot crown spread, which beats the Senator's 56-foot crown.

But wait a minute, complained Florida's tree fan club. That big-butted cypress in the bayou is really two trees that have grown together. Untrue, say the Louisiana defenders; the Cat Island tree is a "multi-stem cypress caused by special genetics." The dispute goes on, with one expert suggesting cutting down both trees, grinding them up, and weighing the sawdust. But rest assured that nobody's going to chop down the Senator.

Searching for the Lost Moon Trees

At the Kennedy Space Center Visitor Complex, in the open area between the exhibit buildings, is a lone 15-foot-tall sycamore. The tree gets little attention from visitors. Most are so caught up in looking at spacecraft that they give no notice to the landscape. But this tree is a piece of our landscape that has been to the moon and back.

In 1971, when Apollo 14 was launched to the moon, the astronauts took a container of sycamore, redwood, Douglas fir, sweet gum, and pine seeds on the voyage. It was part science experiment—to see how the seeds would be affected by a trip to the moon—and part publicity stunt. Upon return from the moon, the seeds were germinated in a laboratory, where they sprouted into normal healthy seedlings.

In 1975, the seedlings were given to the White House, the Space Center, Valley Forge, Independence Hall, and many other educational and historic sites. Today, the moon trees are fully grown. However—and this is pretty weird—no one

kept good records of the locations, so we don't know where most of the trees are. Presently, only forty have been found, and there's an ongoing quest to find the others. Five are in Florida: the one at the Kennedy Space Center, two in Tallahassee, one in Perry, and one in Gainesville.

Moorehaven's Lone Cypress

In Moorehaven, on the western side of Lake Okeechobee, you'll find the Lone Cypress, a living part of South Florida's past. In 1881, the state wanted to drain part of the Everglades. It was not an environmentally smart idea, but they did it anyway. State officials made a deal with a wealthy northerner, Hamilton Disston, to pump out the water in return for a share of the reclaimed land. One of Disston's projects involved digging a canal to connect Lake Okeechobee with the Caloosahatchee River. At the head of this canal, on Lake Okeechobee, was a cypress tree. In 1917, a lock was constructed at the canal entrance, but the Lone Cypress remained as a landmark, a navigational guide for boatmen on the lake. The cypress is still there, and next to it is a plaque that explains its historical significance.

Florida's 800-Year-Old Building

Built 300 Years Before Columbus Discovered the New World!

It's on the Dixie Highway in North Miami, and at eight hundred years old, it's the oldest building in America. Often referred to as the "Old Spanish Monastery," its actual name is "Ancient Spanish Monastery Cloisters," and it is located at St. Bernard de Clairvaux Episcopal Church.

You may be wondering, How was a building constructed in wild Florida three hundred years before Columbus? The answer is that it wasn't built in Florida. It was built in Sacramenia, Spain, between 1133 and 1144, and was originally called the "Monastery of Our Lady, Queen of the Angels." Cistercian monks occupied the building for seven hundred years. In the 1830s, during a social revolution in Spain, it was converted into a granary and stable. But the really interesting part of the story is what happened next.

In 1925, William Randolph Hearst, who liked to shop for big things,

purchased the monastery and dismantled the whole works stone by stone. It was a mammoth undertaking, and two sawmills were built just to produce the eleven thousand shipping crates. Each block was numbered and packed with hay in a crate. The crates were numbered corresponding to the blocks inside and then shipped to the United States. However, at that time, there was an outbreak of hoof-and-mouth disease in Spain, so U.S. Customs officials quarantined the blocks, fearing that the hay could be carrying the disease. The crates were opened, and the hay was burned. A big problem occurred when workmen repacked the crates. Not being particularly fussy kinds of guys, they put the stones in the wrong crates. The entire shipment was then stored in a New York warehouse, where it remained for twenty-six years.

In the meantime, Hearst experienced financial problems and was forced to sell the whole works. In 1952, two men purchased the blocks of stone and moved them to Florida. They intended to reassemble the monastery and make it a tourist attraction. The mismatched crates and blocks turned out to be a giant and very expensive jigsaw puzzle. It took twenty-three men ninety days just to open all the crates, some weighing over a ton. As an example of how big this project was, when the crates were burned, more than seven tons of nails were salvaged from the ashes. Nineteen months and $1.5 million later, the ancient building was reconstructed. The total cost of putting it together was much more than the two nearly bankrupt investors had bargained for, so once again, the monastery was sold, this time to the St. Bernard de Clairvaux Church.

Today, the Ancient Spanish Monastery looks very much like it did eight hundred years ago. It still has the original baptismal font and the iron bell that once called the monks to dinner, and on each stone block you can still see the original stonemason's mark that identifies the person who had cut the block. The ancient monastery is surrounded by beautiful and serene landscaping, with walkways and fountains. It's no wonder that it is a popular place for wedding photographs or private meditation.

Bradenton's Miracle on a Wall

Is it a miracle or something else? The face of Jesus can really be seen on the brick wall of the Palma Sola Presbyterian Church in Bradenton. Although it is visible all the time, it is especially prominent when the wall is wet.

Clearwater's Miracle on a Window

On December 17, 1996, a woman walked out of this bank building on Highway 19 in Clearwater, turned toward the glass front, and saw an iridescent image of the Virgin Mary. The story hit the press, and soon people were flocking by the thousands to witness the miracle. The building became an international religious attraction and was purchased by the Shepherds of Christ Ministries of Ohio. The parking lot became a shrine, where people came to worship and leave offerings. The image was vandalized when someone threw a liquid solution on the glass, which a rainstorm later washed off. Then in the early-morning hours of March 1, 2004, a vandal using a slingshot fired ball bearings at the image, knocking out the three glass panes containing the head and halo. A teenage boy was later arrested, and he admitted to the deed. Although only the lower part of the image is visible now, the building remains a shrine.

Tallest Cross in Florida

Towering 208 feet above Matanzas Bay in St. Augustine, this metallic cross is the largest religious cross in Florida. It marks the spot where Spanish explorers landed in the New World on September 8, 1565, and planted the first cross of Christianity. It was here also that in 1615 the Mission of Nombre de Dios was established. You can still visit the chapel, but it is not as old as you might think. It was built in 1915. The original chapel was damaged during an attack on St. Augustine and later wiped out by a hurricane. The tall cross is lit up at night and is open to the public.

America's Smallest Post Office: Zip Code 34141

On the western edge of the Everglades, in Ochopee, Florida, four hundred postal customers are served by the nation's smallest post office. It was originally built in 1934 as a toolshed for the Gaunt tomato farm. The first post office was in the general store, but when it burned down in 1953, Postmaster Sid Brown began storing and sorting the mail in the toolshed. A short time later, the shed became Ochopee's official post office. The tiny structure measures only ten feet six inches in height, eight feet four inches in width, and seven feet three inches in length. Local folks have resisted attempts by the U.S. Postal Service to replace their famous little post office. It's the biggest attraction in town.

World's Smallest Police Station

Carrabelle on Florida's Gulf Coast, just across the bay from Apalachicola, has the world's smallest police station, the size of a phone booth. That's because it was converted from one in 1963. The town had only two police cars, and when one was on patrol, the other sat by the phone booth. Arrested criminals were taken over the bridge to the Apalachicola jail. A few years ago, Carrabelle built a larger police station but has kept the original one at the corner of Highway 30 and Meridian Street. Locals say it's the most photographed place in town.

Castle Otttis

Driving down the East Coast on A1A from Jacksonville to St. Augustine, you'll see a King Arthur–style castle jutting up from the windswept trees. This is Castle Otttis—that's correct, with three t's—representing, according to locals, the three crosses on Calvary, the hill where Christ was crucified. The castle was built in the 1980s by a Rusty Ickes and Ottis Sadler without plans and, according to a newspaper article, without a permit. The county property appraiser had a problem trying to figure out how to classify the structure, and it was finally listed as a garage because the interior was not finished and there were no utilities. The castle serves as a chapel and is open one Sunday each month.

Ice-Cream Cone

You'll never guess what this place sells. This big ice-cream cone is in Kissimmee.

Ocala's Painted Horses

Ocala is Florida's horse country, and scattered all over town are 52 artistic life-size horses. Crafted from fiberglass, each horse has a name and a crazy paint job done by local artists. Some of these steeds have psychedelic decorations, while other designs are almost three-dimensional. Originally, the horses were part of an art exhibition called "Horse Fever," sponsored by the Florida Thoroughbred Breeders' and Owners' Association. After the exhibition, the colorful equines were auctioned off, and now they stand in front of businesses and residences and in the city park.

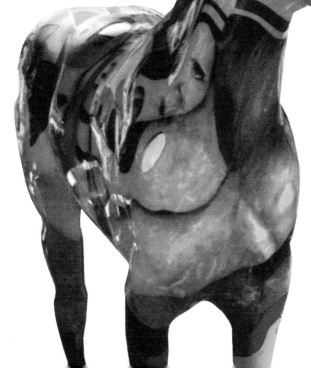

Lincoln Memorial

No, this Lincoln Memorial isn't in Washington, D.C. It's a smaller-scale model that sits in front of the House of Presidents in Clermont, Florida.

Big Cement Gators

At one time, there was an unofficial contest to see which tourist attraction could build the biggest cement alligator. The results are all over the state. There's a 124-foot gator with a Land Rover in its jaws at Kissimmee's defunct Jungleland Zoo. Up the road, near Orlando, is the famous entrance to Gatorland through the toothy creature's open mouth. The biggest concrete gator, 220 feet from snout to tail tip, is Swampy at Jungle Adventures on Highway 50, between Orlando and Titusville.

Big Dolphins

These big dolphins are in front of the Dolphin Research Center on Grassy Key. You probably think it's Flipper and a youngster. Actually, there were five dolphins used in the famous television series *Flipper*. The one best known as "Flipper" was really named "Mitzi." She died in 1972 and is buried at the research center. If you have the money, you can swim with dolphins at the center.

Giant Lobster

This is an impressive sight. It's a thirty-foot lobster in front of the Treasure Harbor Trading Company on Plantation Key. It's made of fiberglass, but the artistic detail is perfect.

Giant Fish

Giant tropical fish on Marathon Key. Scuba divers must be glad that the real ones aren't this big.

Wooden Chiefs

These huge wooden carvings sit beside U.S. 1 between Edgewater and Oak Hill. They are in front of the workshop of wood artist Peter Wolf. Usually, they are standing upright on their own, but this photo was taken two days after Hurricane Charley, a reminder that Mother Nature has no respect for anything, not even great art.

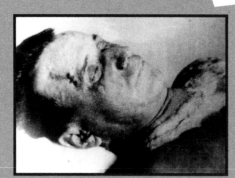

The Barker Gang House

Actually, this isn't the real house. It's only a façade mounted on a trailer frame that's used by the Lake Weir Chamber of Commerce for the annual reenactment of the shootout that ended Ma Barker's gang. With the FBI looking for them, Ma Barker and her sons found refuge in the small town of Ocklawaha, where they rented a house on Lake Weir. But FBI agents were tipped off about their hideout, and on the morning of January 16, 1935, fifteen lawmen surrounded the house and opened fire. It was called the longest gun battle in FBI history, lasting four hours, with more than three thousand rounds of ammunition being fired into the house. When it was over, Ma Barker and her son Fred were dead. In January of each year, the annual Ocklawaha Shootout event is held to commemorate the end of the Barker gang and to salute law enforcement.

ERECTED IN GRATEFUL RECOGNITION OF THE ROLE THE
NORTH AMERICAN POSSUM. A MAGNIFICIENT SURVIVOR OF
THE MARSUPIAL FAMILY PRE-DATING THE AGES OF THE
MASTADON AND THE DINOSAUR. HAS PLAYED IN FURNISHING
BOTH FOOD AND FUR FOR THE EARLY SETTLERS AND THEIR
SUCCESSORS. THEIR PRESENCE HERE HAS PROVIDED A SOURCE
OF NUTRITIOUS AND FLAVORFUL FOOD IN NORMAL TIMES AND
HAS BEEN IMPORTANT AID TO HUMAN SURVIVAL IN TIMES OF
DISTRESS AND CRITICAL NEED.

THE 1982 SESSION OF THE FLORIDA LEGISLATURE
FURTHER RECOGNIZED THE POSSUM BY PASSING A JOINT
RESOLUTION PROCLAIMING THE FIRST SATURDAY IN AUGUST
AS POSSUM DAY IN THE GREAT STATE OF FLORIDA.

ERECTED
BY
WAUSAU COMMUNITY DEVELOP[MENT]
AUG. 7, 1982

DESIGNED AND EREC[TED]
SAPP MEMORIAL,
COTTONDALE FL.

Possum Monument

In the northwestern Florida community of Wausau stands a tall granite monument dedicated to the possum. The marsupial memorial honors the possum for providing food and fur to humans during hard times. In 1982, the Florida legislature passed a joint resolution proclaiming the first Saturday in August as "Florida's Possum Day." Wausau celebrates the day each year with a Possum Festival and the election of a Possum King and Queen. The festivities are held at an arena called Wausau's Possum Palace. We would assume that if they serve possum, it comes with sweet potatoes.

Watch Out for Panthers

Driving across the Everglades on the Tamiami Trail, you'll see several panther crossings. Although these big cats are scarce, they occasionally come in close contact with humans. Near a remote campground on the edge of Big Cypress National Preserve, a rogue panther recently killed several goats, an emu, and a half-dozen chickens. Guess that shows that Florida is still a wild place.

PANTHER CROSSING NEXT 3 MILES

What Happened to Bongoland?

Just a few blocks west of U.S. 1, in Port Orange, you'll find the Dunlawton Sugar Mill ruins. It was here in 1948 that M. D. Lawrence had constructed several life-size concrete dinosaurs for an early tourist attraction called Bongoland. The theme park had a train that was converted from an old truck and that hauled visitors around. The main features were a replica of a Seminole Indian village, a few animals, the historic sugar mill ruins, a human sundial that you stood on and observed your shadow, and a collection of prehistoric "monsters." Compared to modern amusement parks, it may have lacked excitement, but it was never crowded, which may be why it closed in 1952.

In recent years, the county purchased the park and turned it into the Dunlawton Sugar Mill Botanical Gardens. It's a free attraction, and best of all, most of the realistic-looking dinosaurs are still scattered about the nature walks within the gardens.

Southernmost Point

There's always a swarm of tourists buzzing around this giant buoy, at the end of Whitehead Street in Key West. It's the southernmost point in the United States, just ninety miles from Cuba. This spot is closer to Havana than it is to Miami. There used to be just a sign here, but some thieving tourists kept stealing it for a souvenir, so in 1983, the buoy was put up. Try to steal that! Actually, this is not the southernmost point. You can walk several feet south of the marker, and the adjacent naval base sticks out much farther south. But for tourists, this marker will have to do.

World's Most Unusual Monument

Kissimmee is where you'll find what is locally billed as the "World's Most Unusual Monument," a fifty-foot-high, irregular quadrilateral pyramid . . . whatever that is. It's called the "Monument of States," and its twenty-one tiers contain fifteen hundred stones and rocks from every state and twenty-two countries. The tall monument, topped off by a 562-pound concrete eagle, was a project of the All States Tourist Club of Kissimmee and was dedicated by the governor on March 28, 1943. But wait! There are more than rocks embedded in this weird monument. Upon close inspection, you'll see a meteorite, a cannonball from Michigan, buffalo horns from Montana, petrified wood from Arizona, a rock from the Sahara, a human skull, glacier eggs, a petrified apple from Wisconsin, and a map of Holland.

Crash Landings?

These pictures might give one pause about the skill of Florida's pilots. Actually, the airplanes are staged attention getters. In Polk City, a cargo plane is stuck nose-first in a cow pasture beside Interstate 4, advertising the Fantasy of Flight museum. In Daytona, a zebra-striped plane appears to have crashed into a safari-themed miniature golf course. And on Highway 1, in Rose Bay, a yellow plane called "Nosy Rosy" has landed on top of a seafood restaurant.

Beer-Can Car

This is a great way to recycle a beer can, provided it's big enough to hold an engine. We might call this speedster the staff car of Sopotnick's Cabbage Patch, a biker hangout in Samsula. The Cabbage Patch is popular among bikers for its coleslaw, but they don't eat it; they wrestle in it. This is where the annual women's coleslaw wrestling matches are held during Bike Week.

Lake Placid: Plants, Clowns, and Talking Murals

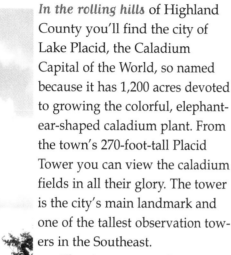

In the rolling hills of Highland County you'll find the city of Lake Placid, the Caladium Capital of the World, so named because it has 1,200 acres devoted to growing the colorful, elephant-ear-shaped caladium plant. From the town's 270-foot-tall Placid Tower you can view the caladium fields in all their glory. The tower is the city's main landmark and one of the tallest observation towers in the Southeast.

The city was once known as Lake Stearns. But in 1927, Dr. Melvil Dewey, the inventor of the Dewey decimal system, renamed it Lake Placid, after his hometown in New York State. Dewey's intention was to transform it into a winter resort for northerners. (It does have twenty-seven lakes.)

Lake Placid has many odd claims to fame. It boasts more clowns per capita than any other Florida city, because it is home to Toby's Clown College, founded by Toby the Clown, a.k.a. Keith Stokes. Toby's clown graduates have long provided free entertainment in area hospitals, schools, and nursing homes.

Lake Placid's entire downtown area is an open-air art gallery. That started with the founding of the Lake Placid Mural Society, whose purpose was to beautify the town by placing murals on many of its buildings. Award-winning artists from all over the state were asked to paint huge murals on just about every wall in town. Several of the murals have realistic sound effects, such as the 175-foot-long painting of a Florida cattle drive featuring the sounds of thunder, cowboy yips, and mooing cows.

The original 1920 jail is on exhibit at the Lake Placid Historical Museum.

The smaller replica of the jail is a trash bin in front of the police station.

More Lake Placid: America's Most Beautiful Trash Cans

The most unusual creations are the city's fifteen trash containers, referred to locally as "streetscape containers." The Mural Society decided they could not allow ugly trash cans to distract from the city's beautiful murals, so the waste containers were designed to look like something else: a steam locomotive, an antique car, a rustic fishing shack, a clown-in-a-box, and whatever else struck the artist's fancy. So if you're in Lake Placid and need to discard a fast-food wrapper, look for the little yellow school bus or the wooden stump—they're really trash containers.

The author next to a trash container disguised as a 1927 Chrysler.

The Weirdest Mailbox in Florida

Glen Bailey of New Smyrna makes no bones about it—he's a biker and a Confederate. The entire roof of his house is painted to look like the Confederate flag. But the weirdest thing about his home is his roadside mailbox—it rests on a big ol' chopper mounted with two skeletons. In addition to surviving several attacks by vandals, his strange mailbox has withstood being hit by cars twice and, believe it or not, by a detached boat trailer that had plowed into it. Glen says that when he first put up the mailbox, the cops tried to make him take it down because they felt it was a traffic hazard. When he refused, local officials attempted to classify it as an abandoned vehicle. But Bailey stood his ground, and his weird mailbox is still receiving mail.

As for his roof, it gets as much attention from passing cars as his unusual mailbox. Glen had measured off his roof and, using templates for the stars, painted it by hand. As a native Floridian, originally from Winter Haven, Glen says it's his way of expressing his southern heritage, adding, "There's no other roof like it in Florida."

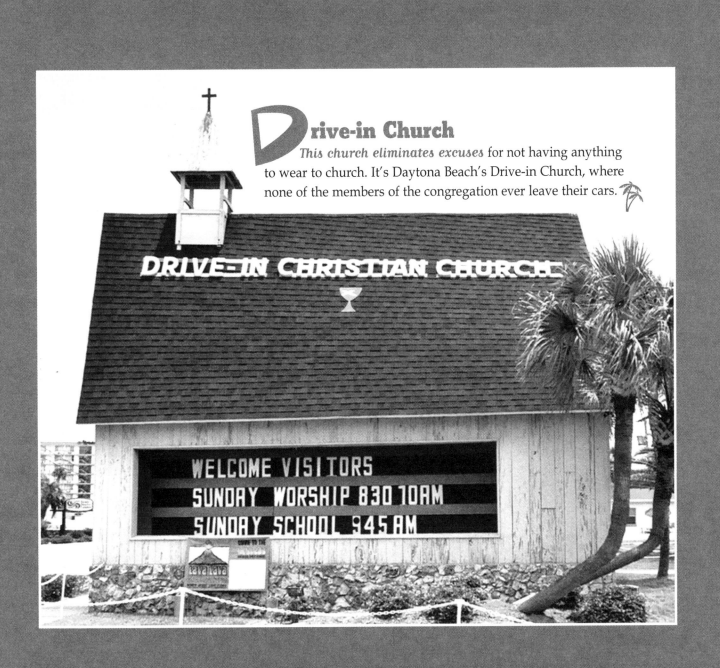

Drive-in Church

This church eliminates excuses for not having anything to wear to church. It's Daytona Beach's Drive-in Church, where none of the members of the congregation ever leave their cars.

DRIVE-IN CHRISTIAN CHURCH

WELCOME VISITORS
SUNDAY WORSHIP 830 10AM
SUNDAY SCHOOL 945 AM

Roads Less Traveled

Florida has many roads, though not enough to keep pace with the state's growing traffic demands. Some roads are fast lanes to tourist destinations, while others are scenic routes for those who want to meander and enjoy the sights. Then there are the detours around reality, roads into paranormal passageways, straight into Florida's weird side. These are the places with legends, the ones with scary lights that chase your car or the ones where gravity is reversed. It's the legends that dare us to travel onto these byways, where nocturnal phantoms ride translucent horses and ghostly screams emanate from the thick roadside woods.

Maybe there is nothing to the tales about these trails, or maybe there is. Hey, we're just passing along a piece of legend. It's up to you whether you want to venture down one of these roads less traveled.

Bloody Bucket Road

Bloody Bucket Road isn't the real name of this sinister road in Wauchula, but that's what everybody calls it because of stories about what had happened there many years ago. Then there is also the Bloody Bucket Bridge, which contributes to the strange tales about this place.

This paved road runs south off Main Street in Wauchula and doesn't look all that threatening in the daytime. But drive farther on and cross the bridge and things start looking a bit different, at least in the moonlight.

The road was once a dirt passageway called Rhinehardt or Reinhart Pass Road and is over a hundred years old. Those are the facts, but the rest of the story comes from locals who profess to have some knowledge about how the road got its creepy name.

Many years ago, a former slave woman came down from Georgia with her husband and settled in Wauchula. She served as the midwife for the community and allegedly delivered several hundred babies. Being concerned that some families had too many children to feed, the woman decided to help out by eliminating a few at birth. She would smother the babies, then take them down to the bridge and bury them in the woods along the river. People became suspicious after the deaths of so many babies delivered by her. Some said she was deranged because she could not have children of her own or because her children had been taken from her when she was a slave.

Whatever the reason, the sensible townsfolk refused to let her deliver any more babies, and soon the woman went truly crazy, perhaps because the souls of the babies had come back to haunt her.

It is claimed that she would sit beside a bucket, which would fill with the blood of all the infants she had killed. She would empty the bucket, but it would fill with blood again. She wore herself out carrying the blood-filled buckets to a bridge, where she would empty them in the river, but still the buckets continued to fill.

One day, while emptying a bucket in the river, the old woman fell in and drowned. For several days following her demise, the river ran red with blood. And so the bridge came to be known as Bloody Bucket Bridge, and the name carried over to the road.

How much of the story is true is hard to determine. There is some evidence that it might have been promoted in a Halloween story by an amateur writer in Wauchula. Whether the writer made up the story or used an existing yarn is not known, but it certainly created momentum for a legend.

Bridge Over Bloody Water

There's a bridge in Wauchula called Bloody Bucket Bridge, and if you go there at certain times and look at the river water, it will be red like blood. This happens only when the moon is full, and you have to go there at night because in the daytime you can't see it. We went there one night just to see if it was true. We shined a flashlight down there, and yes, the water was as red as blood. My friend said it was because of the tannic acid from tree roots that grow along the river, but I don't think so. It is much too red for tannic acid. There is a story about people pouring blood in the river but I don't know if it was human or cow or some other blood.—*Michele1979*

Cries from the Blood Bucket Woods

On Halloween night in 2003, we parked near the canoe launching place and walked down that road called Bloody Bucket just to see if we could see anything. It is really a scary place, and I don't advise anybody with a faint heart to go down there at night. There are sounds that come out of the woods by the river that sound like children crying. There is a story that a woman killed her babies and buried them in the woods right where we heard the sounds. We stood very still and tried to listen to see if we could make them out. One of the guys said it could be birds roosting in the trees, but the rest of us did not think so—it sounded too much like crying. As we were standing there, something ran out of the woods and crossed the road. We ran back to the car and got out of there. There is something real strange on that road.—*buddyX*

No Peace for Peace River

Here's something that I got from a friend in Avon Park. It is called Bloody Bucket Road down in Wauchula. A weird story if there ever was one. There was an old midwife that lived on this road, and she went crazy and started killing the babies that she delivered and throwing them in the river. The Peace River runs under this road, and that is where she threw them. One day she drowned in the river, and they say that you can hear her screaming for help and hear the babies crying that she killed. You might want to check it out.—*Mr Xfiles*

Buckets and Buckets and Buckets of Blood

A long time ago, there was an old black slave woman who was a midwife in Wauchula. She got caught putting her hand over babies' mouths and killing them. She was burying the babies in the woods beside this road called Bloody Bucket Road. The blood part came from her dumping buckets of blood in the river. It was said that she visualized her buckets filling up with blood, and she would empty them in the river, then wash them out, only for them to immediately fill up again. After she died, her husband said that when she did this, he would look in the buckets, and there was never any blood; she just thought there was blood. She ran herself to death carrying those empty buckets and dumping imaginary blood in the river, probably because she was driven insane for killing those babies. Of course, I don't know that she even killed any babies; it could be only a story. But that is the Bloody Bucket Road tale.

—*Cynthia*

Haunting of Rolling Acres Road

This road crosses Highway 441 in Lady Lake, and if you turn east on it, you will be disappointed. It runs through a populated area of ordinary residences and businesses—nothing weird at all. But in the other direction, the scene is a little different. The road goes up and down rolling hills and eventually passes through a wooded section just before crossing a main road and coming to a dead end. We asked a local man if he had ever heard any stories about the road being haunted by a mysterious lady in white or perhaps by a man in black—the stories vary. He told us that he had heard "Halloween yarns" about teenagers seeing ghosts on the road and hearing strange noises in the woods. He also added that he thought "it was just boys hiding in the trees trying to scare some other kids." Whatever the origin, the story seems to have a firm footing in Florida folklore.

Terrifying Sounds

In Lady Lake, there is a haunted road, called Rolling Hills Road or something like that, where a ghost lady walks the road at night and terrifying sounds come out of the woods. The story is that her name is Julie and that she was murdered by a jealous lover after she decided to marry another man; now she walks the road at night.

—Michele 1979

Woman Dressed in White

Oh yeah, it is true about Rolling Acres Road, because we went there to check it out. You won't hear anything unless you park your car and turn off the engine; then roll down your windows, and you can hear sounds like banshees in the woods. I used to live in Fruitland Park, and I know a bunch of kids that had unusual experiences on that road. One dude went out there and said that they seen a woman dressed in white or glowing, and it was like you could see through her.*—Tim*

Car Mysteriously Stalls

On Rolling Acres Road in Lady Lake, you can hear very loud roars coming from the woods, and there's a bright light in the shape of a woman that can be seen there. The ghost that haunts this road is a murdered woman named Julia. All I know is that our ghost group went there to check it out, and the car we were in stalled. It took better than ten minutes to get it cranked. I think it had something to do with that road.

—ghostbusters

Black Hooded Shadow Guy

My boyfriend told me about Rolling Hills Road, so I said for him to take me there so we could see for ourselves if there's anything to it. It is a hard-surface road that goes up and down a few steep hills, but near the end, there are some pastures and woods, and this is where we saw a something or somebody dressed in black with a hood that made him look like the grim reaper standing on the side of the road. This was at night, so we didn't stop to ask who he was, but we drove past and turned around at the dead end, and when we came back, that black shadow guy was gone. He had to either vanish or hide in the woods.*—Melanie N.*

When the horse died, it required a tractor to haul his heavy corpse out of the stable to his burial pit beside Celery Avenue.

Phantom Horse of Celery Avenue

Celery Avenue runs between the Saint Johns River and the town of Sanford. Before 1940, this was the celery capital of the nation, and both sides of this avenue were lined with acres of celery fields. The east end of the road cuts through old Indian grounds, where there is still a well-preserved burial mound. For years, we have heard stories about a phantom horse on this road, but the only historical account connected to a horse is on the west end. It is in this area where a giant horse is allegedly buried beneath the road.

The big horse, which stood twenty-two hands high and weighed 3,200 pounds, belonged to a local blacksmith named Sligh Earnest. When the horse died, it required a tractor to haul his heavy corpse out of the stable to his burial pit beside Celery Avenue. Since that time, the road has been widened several times, and the horse's grave has been covered over. Whether this indignity to an equine has anything to do with the phantom-horse story is anybody's guess. But there are stories....

The Horse Vanished

This guy I know in Orlando told me about seeing a white horse that vanished running on the road in Sanford. I think it was on that road that goes east and west by that old stadium. He just said that he saw this white horse galloping beside his car, and it followed him for a short distance, and while he was watching it and trying to steer the car, the horse just like vanished.—*Anonymous*

Translucent Warrior on a White Horse

I live in Altamonte, and one day a friend of mine was coming to see me. She was driving down that road from the Osteen Bridge to Sanford, because the traffic is easier. Anyway, she did not want to ask about what she saw, because she thought it would sound crazy, so she asked me to tell you. It was about 9 or 9:30, and she was driving down that road and noticed something to her right on the side of the road. She turned and looked and said that what she saw was a pure white horse with an Indian on his back, and the Indian had a long feathered headdress on. She said it was, like, translucent; it was white, but you could see through it. It ran along beside her car for about a quarter of a mile and just vanished. She said that she was doing about 40 and whatever it was kept up with her speed. Have you ever heard of any ghosts on this road or has anybody else ever said anything about seeing something like this?—*Linda*

It Did Not Seem Like a Solid Horse

Okay, this is going to sound nuts, but I know what I saw. I was going down Celery Avenue coming back from the beach, and it was dark. I was about halfway down the road when a big white horse dashed across in front of my car. It did not seem like a solid horse; what I mean is that I thought I could see through it. I've thought about it; maybe it was a trick of my headlights, but the horse was real. I hit the brakes and looked quickly in the direction of where he had gone, but did not see him. I don't know if it was a ghost or what, but I saw something strange.—*Robin*

agnolia Creek Lane

Several miles south of Montverde, on the west side of Lake Apopka, is a narrow road that accommodates only one car at a time. It is partially paved and goes through a heavily wooded area.

According to legend, the road is haunted by two hundred passengers who had been killed in a major train wreck. While the road does appear to be built on an old railroad bed, the only documented railroad ran slightly north of this location. We have found no proof that a train wreck ever occurred anywhere near this road, and even if it had, it's doubtful that it would have been a passenger train. Still, such details rarely discourage the legend tellers, and many insist that very strange noises come from these woods.

Ghostly Noises in the Woods

Magnolia Creek Lane is where all kinds of horrible things happened back in the 1890s, which accounts for all the stories I heard from people, who told me about frightening noises back in the woods along this road. I went there, but there's a lot of new houses there now, so it's not as wild as it used to be, but it still has a thick forest of oaks.–*Brian*

Wrecked Souls Still Haunt the Woods

The Magnolia Creek Road is where a railroad used to be. This was way back when there were steam engines, so I don't really know what year it was; anyway, there was a big train wreck that happened on this railroad that killed two hundred people. It was the biggest train wreck in Florida, and their souls still haunt the wooded areas where the old rails used to be. I think you can find something about the wreck in Winter Garden railroad museum.–*big-potato*

You Can Hear Screams

There's a creek that runs to Lake Apopka, and that's where that train wreck happened. Along this creek you can hear screams. I went back in there years ago with a buddy, and you can hear loud screams in the woods, but when you try to get near them, they move farther away. They say it's screams from the train crew that died, but it could be sound that is being reflected from someplace else, because there is a big lake near there and doesn't water carry sound?–*Shooter*

Shadows of People Walking the Road

My cousin went to Montverde Academy and heard about this road that runs off 455 that used to be a railroad bed; they say that if you go down there at night, you can hear ghostly sounds and see eerie shadows of people walking on the road. I don't know for sure about this, because I never went there, so it is just what I heard.–*Michele19*

Suicide Road

This strange road off Route 3 in the Merritt Island National Wildlife Refuge has somehow acquired the reputation of a suicide road. The road, which has no official name or number, was evidently built many decades ago and is only about a mile long, with two or three turns before it reaches a dead end. Actually, there seems to be no logical reason for this road to exist. According to the ghastly tale, someone committed suicide here fifty-some years ago and you can still see the blood. Weird Florida could find nothing concerning a suicide or death of any kind on this road. However, there are some red spots of glossy paint (or is it paint?) on the pavement, which at first glance looks just like blood. The spots are definitely startling if you are looking for evidence of the suicide story.

Also Called "Dead Man Road"

Suicide road is also called "dead man road." There was a man that committed suicide on this road before it became government property. They say that when it rains, the spot where he died turns red like blood. It is very hard to find this place because it is off the main road. –*Shooter*

You'll Get Sucked Dry of Blood

We went out there and checked out Suicide Road, and it is not easy to find. Somebody just built a road to nowhere in the middle of nowhere. Why it's there is the biggest mystery of all. It's like they were practicing building a road. Beware that if you go there, you will be sucked dry of blood by the horrendous swarms of mosquitoes. –*Willlis-in-Titusville*

Possible Origin of the Story

I asked one of the security officers that patrol the wildlife refuge about Suicide Road, and he said he never heard of it. I think the story got started by a man that had a fish camp there a long time ago, and after the government took all that land he had to move. When I went to high school, our coach told us the story about it and said that he got it from that guy that had a fish camp there, but did not know if anybody really committed suicide there. –*pottymouth*

Road Up Spook Hill

Spook Hill is a long-promoted gravity-defying hill in the city of Lake Wales, where you can park your car at the bottom and it will roll uphill. It is such a popular place for curiosity seekers that the city has put up little brown direction signs all over town so you can find the mysterious hill. However, watch out, because local pranksters often turn these signs so they point in the opposite direction. It takes only one switched sign to send you off into oblivion. If you can get to Spook Hill Elementary School, you'll see a hill just ahead of you. Once at this point, you cannot miss the sign erected by the city that explains the history of the place. The sign also explains how to experience Spook Hill: Park your car on the white line that's painted on the street, shift to neutral, and let her roll up the hill.

We carefully followed the instructions, and within a second, the car was gliding very slowly uphill—or at least that's what it seemed to be doing. If you go there on a weekend, you could see as many as fifteen to twenty cars at one time waiting to experience the crazy gravity.

There are several stories about how Spook Hill was discovered. The most popular account has to do with a black gentleman who parked his automobile at the base of the hill to do a little fishing in a nearby lake. He had hardly reached the lake when he turned and saw his car rolling up the hill. Thus began a tale that circulated within the black community for years and eventually found its way into local white folklore.

Other accounts say that the hill was a sacred spot used by early Native Americans for religious ceremonies. One story even claimed that there was a huge magnetic rock buried within the hill, which is similar to another tale, blaming the weird effects on a magnetic meteorite that hit the earth at this spot and is still buried inside the hill. History speaks about early pioneers noticing that their horses had to labor hard to go down Spook Hill but found it easy going up the hill.

So what does the state geologist have to say about Spook Hill? Some time ago we received the following in response to our question about the strange phenomenon: "There are no mysterious forces at work at Spook Hill. It is an illusion and can be verified with a simple carpenter's level." Don't you just love these smarty britches who always ruin a good mystery with scientific mishmash?

Okay, so we took a carpenter's level to Spook Hill

and discovered that what was "up" was really "down." The lay of the terrain around Spook Hill is responsible for the illusion. If you approach the hill from the opposite direction and survey the surroundings, you can see how the illusion works. Cars are not really rolling uphill; they are actually rolling downhill. Got it? Knowing the secret really doesn't spoil the fun, because you can still have a good time figuring out the illusion.

Trick of the Land

I know everybody believes Spook Hill is just a trick of the land, but what explains the fact that not only do cars roll uphill but also soda cans, oranges, or anything else that is, like, round?–*Sherry Lynn*

Is Something Wrong with the Hill?

I don't think Spook Hill works anymore, because I parked my car like the sign says to do and nothing happened. Do you know if anything is wrong with it?–*Anonymous*

Weird Feeling

Instead of using your vehicle to check out Spook Hill, try walking or running up or down the hill––it's a weird feeling, because when you are going what seems to be downhill, it is harder than when you are going uphill.–*Randy*

Does Time Run Slower at Spook Hill?

You know Spook Hill in Lake Wales, where cars roll up the hill? I heard that your watch will run slower on this hill and that you can watch the second hand slow down.–*Kbar*

Greenbriar Light Road

The real name for this road is just Greenbriar Road, and it runs east of Switzerland, Florida. Yep, that's really the name of this peaceful little hamlet in Saint Johns County, but don't expect to see any Alps in this Switzerland.

On Greenbriar Road, there is a light that chases cars. It looks like the headlight of a motorcycle, and according to reports, it usually follows behind a car at a distance of about three hundred feet. Although the mysterious ball of light never passes a car, it has been known to sit atop a vehicle until reaching a certain point on the road, whereupon it vanishes.

In 1987, the light grabbed the interest of several science experts, who went there to determine what it was. That same year, the Saint Johns County Sheriff's Department also investigated reports about the weird light. Investigations could come up with no explanation. It is not an area that would normally produce swamp gas, as in other cases involving ghost-light phenomena. According to folklore, the light is supposed to be the headlight of a young phantom motorcyclist. Racing on the road one night, he lost control of his bike and was decapitated by a guy wire supporting a telephone pole. Why this particular mode of dying would attract the light to cars is not explained—only the cyclist knows that.

We went to Greenbriar Road to check it out and were a little disappointed. It's not at the location described in various books, nor was it a dirt road. It is a fairly heavily traveled asphalt road. Since we visited during the daytime, we had no encounters with a ball of light, although other people claim to have been pursued by this weird phenomenon.

We turned around and went back, but didn't see anything. I really think we saw a ghost of that guy that was killed on his motorcycle on that road.

Repeated Encounters with the Light

Everybody knew about the strange light out on Greenbriar Road, so we went there to see if we could see it. We did see it but at first thought it was a one-eyed car coming down the road. It did not move toward us very fast. We were facing it, and it kind of came up about a tenth of a mile in front of our car and just sat there, wavering or hovering over the road. We were facing east, and we turned around in the middle of the road, and when we started driving toward the west, we looked behind us, and the light was following our car. Just before we got to the end of Greenbriar Road, it disappeared. We turned around and went back, and sure enough, it popped up way down the road and again came to about a tenth of a mile in front and hovered again. We repeated this four times, and each time, the light did the same thing. We tried to figure out what it was, but we have no idea. It looked about the size of a basketball and glowed pretty bright, not hazy or faint, but a very bright whitish glow.—*Paul R.*

Light Comes Out of Nowhere

There is a road in St. Johns County that runs off Road 13 between Fruit Cove and Switzerland and is called Greenbriar Road. There is a ghost light on this road that appears out of nowhere, and it will follow your car. I saw this light with my friend Frank, who told me about it. It is supposed to be the ghost of a guy that was killed while riding his bike on the road, and the light is the headlight of his bike.—*Jason*

Was Told to Leave the Area

Me and three other dudes went to Greenbriar Road to check out that light that chases cars. We were sitting there in the dark on the side of the road waiting to see it, and after being there about thirty minutes, we saw not one, but two lights coming at us. It turned out to be a deputy sheriff, who stopped and asked us what we were doing sitting there in the dark on the side of the road. We told him we were looking for a ghost light. He thought we were crazy and ordered us to move on. So if you go there, beware that the cops will tell you to leave.—*Jim S.*

Phantom Motorcyclist

A few years ago, I went to see Greenbriar Road at night with three of my friends. We had heard the stories about that light that people see, and we wanted to see it. We drove up and down the road for like forty minutes trying to see something, but never saw anything until we got ready to leave. My friend Tom was driving, and he looked in the rearview mirror and said what is that? We looked behind us, and there was the headlight of a motorcycle coming up fast. We slowed down a little and thought that the biker would pass us, but then just as it got right behind us about a hundred feet, the light went out. There was no motorcycle or anything. We turned around and went back, but didn't see anything. I really think we saw a ghost of that guy that was killed on his motorcycle on that road.—*Todd M.*

It's Swamp Gas

I have never seen the Greenbriar Light, but my cousin who lives in Green Cove Springs said that he did and that it is only swamp gas. The light is greenish yellow and drifts up out of a low area, and you can't see it but at certain times of the year.—*Shooter*

i-4 Dead Zone

Halfway between Daytona and Orlando is a quarter-mile section of Interstate 4 known to locals as the "Dead Zone." This short span of asphalt, located in Seminole County at the south end of the interstate bridge across the St. Johns River, has become legendary for its high number of traffic accidents. Depending on sources, there have been an estimated 1,048 to 1,740 car crashes at this location since the highway was opened in 1963, a significant number of which involved fatalities. State officials blamed traffic congestion for the unusually high number of crashes, but others have attributed the cause to something more sinister. To understand the basis for the I-4 Dead Zone legend, we need to take a trip back in time.

Prior to 1880, this area was an untamed wilderness, part of a large grant owned by Henry Sanford, head of the Florida Land and Colonization Company. In 1886, the area was divided into ten-acre parcels in a scheme to start a Roman Catholic community called Saint Joseph's Colony. Sanford believed that he could unload some real estate quickly by attracting Catholic immigrants from Germany to his colony. He appointed a priest, Felix Swembergh, to oversee the plan. However, according to central Florida historian Christine Kinlaw-Best, the effort got off to a bad start: Only four immigrant families settled there, and in 1887, there was an outbreak of yellow fever, which wiped out four members of one immigrant family.

At the time, Father Swembergh was away in Tampa, attending to other fever victims. (He eventually succumbed to the disease himself.) Fearing that the fever was contagious, others buried the bodies of the immigrants in the woods, with no last rites and no priest in attendance.

By 1890, Saint Joseph's Colony had evolved into the rural town of Lake Monroe, named after the local lake. Part of the land was cleared for farming, except for the tiny cemetery where the bodies of the immigrant family lay. When Albert S. Hawkins bought the land in 1905, the graves sat like an island in the middle of a cultivated field, but time had erased the names on the four wooden markers.

The origin of the graves had long since been lost, but local tradition said the burials were of a "Dutch family who had died from the fever." According to accounts, Mr. Hawkins leased his land to other farmers and warned them not to tamper with the little burial plot, a warning that required heeding. One farmer tried to remove the rusty wire fence surrounding the graves, and on the same day, his house burned down. Weird things also happened in the Hawkins home, which stood at the edge of the field. Allegedly, the home burned down after Hawkins, ignoring his own warning, removed the nearly rotted wooden markers. After Mrs. Hawkins blamed the fire on the graves, Mr. Hawkins quickly replaced the markers.

With all the weird shenanigans, the Hawkins field became known locally as the "Field of the Dead." In 1959, the farm was purchased by the government to make way for Interstate 4. During the survey for the right-of-way, the four nameless graves were marked for relocation. However, bureaucracies being what they are, the graves were never moved. In September 1960, fill dirt was dumped atop them to elevate the new highway.

This is where history gets weird. At this same instant, Hurricane Donna slammed into South Florida and plowed its way across the tip of Florida toward the Gulf of Mexico. Then, on the very day that the graves were covered with fill dirt, Donna changed direction near Tampa and headed northeastward across the peninsula. Strangely enough, her deadly path paralleled the surveyed route of the new highway. The big storm's eye passed over the graves at midnight on September 10, 1960. Donna's fury, the worst experienced in central Florida in generations, halted highway construction for nearly a month.

On the day that Interstate 4 was opened to traffic, a tractor-trailer truck hauling a load of frozen shrimp became the Dead Zone's first casualty when it mysteriously went out of control and jackknifed right above the graves. That was the beginning of a weird legacy of accidents that continue to this day. In recent accounts, people claim their cell phones will not work or that static disrupts their radios in this section of highway. A few have claimed encounters at night with wispy balls of light that zigzag just above the pavement. Is it payback time for the dead, or have people's imaginations gone wild? Whatever the case, locals swear there's something sinister at work here, and it may be caused by an eerie secret just beneath the asphalt.

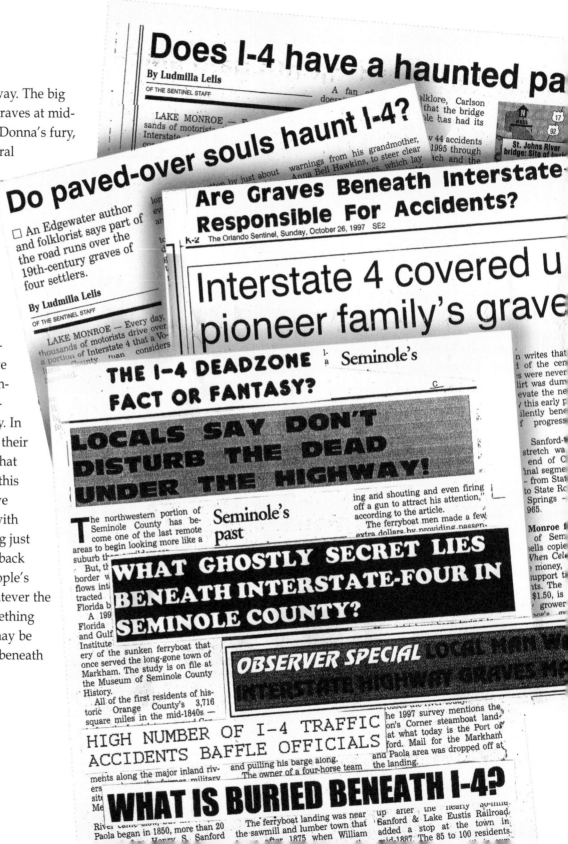

Will Never Drive on I-4 Again

I always heard about this strange part of the highway but did not believe it until I had two accidents right in the middle of the dead zone: two different accidents in two different months. I will never drive I-4 again. I don't know if this is caused by spirits or some other anomaly, but it is too dangerous in that spot. You are more likely to be hurt in the dead zone than by some terrorist act. I encourage everyone to read about the dead zone and make up your own minds. I plan to steer clear of the place.—*Scotty*

Dead Zone Kills Cell Phones Too

One explanation you haven't considered for "dead spots" like the one on I-4 is limestone deposits close to the surface. My grandfather, an engineer, tells me that limestone absorbs radio waves. I have found personally that many of the local spots where I lose my cell phone signal have large limestone deposits. Anyway, it's something to consider.—*Kyrie*

Another Dead Zone Accident

I never knew about that haunted spot on Interstate 4 until I looked at this site. I say I never knew, but have experienced it because the only car accident I ever had happened right where those graves are, and what is really eerie is my steering wheel locked for no good reason, causing me to crash into the guard rail and tore up the whole side of my Buick. So I am a true believer of the I-4 Dead Zone and warn others to take heed. It really exists; there is something weird about that area!—*J. Collins*

Will Avoid Dead Zone at All Costs

I just read about the I-4 dead zone. Being new to Florida, I had no idea about the graves. My daughter and I are sensitives. We get very uncomfortable and almost frightened when we drive over that area—so much so that I avoid it at all costs, even if I have to drive 20 miles out of my way. Now I know why.—*Bambi*

Sensitive to a Presence in the Dead Zone

I visit Florida frequently, riding my motorcycle down from S.C. I guess you can say I'm "sensitive" to paranormal things, to a point anyway. I usually can feel and sense a presence more often than actually seeing it. I've been on I-4 MANY times and have felt something riding over that bridge and in the surrounding area.—*Dano*

Another Dead Zone Victim

I read about that Dead Zone spot on Interstate 4 near the St. Johns River. Believe it or not, the last two times that I vacationed in Central Florida, I had a car accident at that very spot. The area is now under construction, but I don't think it will change things—there is something very strange about that section.—*Johnnie L.*

The Secret That Lies Beneath

Anybody ever hear about the I-4 dead zone up between Orlando and Deland, near the St. Johns River? There is a half-mile section of I-4 that is supposedly haunted because there is a family cemetery that is covered up by the highway. There have been over a thousand traffic deaths there in the past few years. The state road department admits to the high incident rate but has covered up the secret that lies beneath the interstate. If you drive on I-4, beware of this area. It is truly haunted, or something really strange is going on there.—*J.K.*

Something Evil About That Part of the Interstate

I believe there is something evil about that part of Interstate 4. I have been involved in three accidents in that place—once as a driver and twice as a passenger in another person's car. But get this: My neighbor's cousin was killed in a motorcycle crash at that same spot a few years ago. Yes indeed, something is paranormal about the I-4 dead zone. They can fix that bridge all they want—but the dead zone will still be there.—*Jan*

Old Red Eyes
of Kingsley Plantation Road

The Kingsley Plantation on St. George Island, northeast of Jacksonville, has a strange past and, according to legend, a wicked red-eyed spirit that has lingered around these parts for nearly two centuries.

Zephaniah Kingsley established this historic plantation on St. George Island in 1813 for the purpose of growing cotton, sugarcane, citrus fruits, and corn. Over time, the planter became quite wealthy and eventually owned 32,000 acres and more than two hundred slaves working for him on four plantations. He had an unusually benevolent relationship with his slaves. They worked under a task system, which meant that once the daily work was

Kingsley plantation house

done, they were free to take care of their own business, like tending their gardens or going fishing. Kingsley even married one of his slaves in an African ceremony, a union that produced three children. His wife, Anna Madgigine Jai, played a major part in the plantation's management and eventually became one of the wealthiest women in East Florida.

When Florida became a U.S. territory in 1821, Kingsley became concerned with federal laws that placed harsh restrictions on slaves and discriminated against free persons of color. This prompted him in 1837 to move his family and slaves to Haiti, where they established their own colony.

The Kingsley plantation house, though, is still standing on twenty-five acres of the original property, along with the ruins of several slave quarters in a half-moon-shaped row. The narrow, unpaved road to the Kingsley house is scenic but a little bumpy and, at the edge of dark, downright frightening.

This is the domain of Old Red Eyes. If you go there, some say, you can see him in your rearview mirror or hear the sounds of his victims in the woods along the road. Old Red Eyes is the wicked spirit of a slave who had raped and killed several of the plantation's female slaves. He was caught by the other slaves and hanged from an oak tree near the entrance to the plantation.

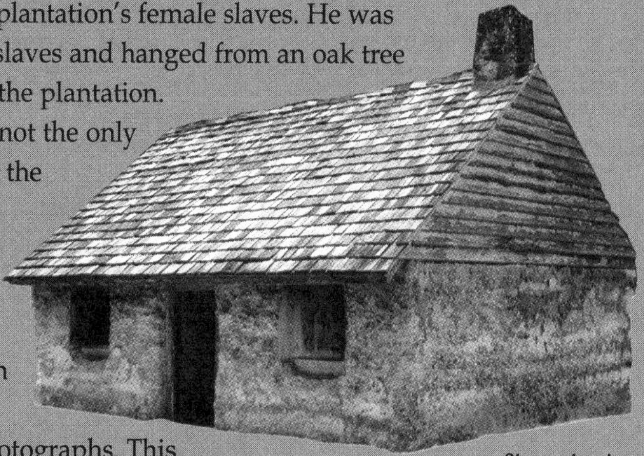

Old Red Eyes is not the only haunting business at the Kingsley Plantation. There are stories about a woman in a white dress seen on the porch of the main house; however, she shows up only in photographs. This ghost is said to be Zephaniah Kingsley's

Slave shack

African wife, Anna. In the yard of the house, you can hear the screams of a child coming from an old well. Allegedly, the child fell into the well and drowned. We checked the well, but heard no screams, perhaps because it now has a heavy cover on it, which prevents ghost hunters from leaning over and falling in.

The eeriest things we witnessed were some twisted trees and vines hanging over the narrow road. Seeing them, one can easily understand how a ghost could be conjured up in these woods, especially if you're driving there at dusk.

Ghostly Peacocks of Kingsley Plantation

We were told about the ghost on the road to the Kingsley Plantation while on the ghost tour on Amelia Island, so on the way home, we drove down that road. It was just before sunset, and the sun was filtering through the branches of the trees on the road. I was looking out in the woods when all of a sudden two totally white peacocks flew right across in front of our car. It scared the heebe-jeebees out of me. I have

Haunted well

never seen white peacocks, only beautiful iridescent ones, but these were albinos. We looked to see where they went and could not see anything. Now I wonder if this has anything to do with the ghost stories about that place.–*Anne T.*

Summertime, When the Red Eyes Are Glowin'

I went there with a carload of friends, and we all saw two red lights following us. It is real, but they say you can only see it in the summer months because that is when that man was hanged there.

–*gopirates22*

Warning: Red Eyes in Mirror
May Be Closer Than They Appear!

I saw Old Red Eyes several years ago. I have a friend that lives just off that road and had taken him home from Jacksonville one night. It was about midnight, and after dropping him off, I was driving back down that road and looked in the side mirror of my car and saw two red lights. At first I thought it was the taillights of another car, but they were too close together. I slowed down a little and watched them in the mirror, and it looked like they were coming closer. I knew that I had not passed another car, and it did not seem like a car would be coming down that dark road backwards. I stopped and stuck my head out the window and looked back, and there was nothing there. Then I looked in the mirror again, and there they were, and they were right behind my car. I gunned it and raced out of there. –*Jan*

Captives Cry from Old Red Eyes' Woods

I think Old Red Eyes' name was Gauntlet Jack or something like that. Anyway, he caused a slave uprising, and he was hanged from a tree on the road that goes to the Kingsley Plantation. He can usually be seen after dark. Most of the people who see him are women, and they only see his eyes following behind their car. In the woods, you can hear people screaming. They say that is the souls of all the people that Red Eyes is holding hostage. I have never seen him, but I have heard weird sounds, like people crying coming out of the woods. I have heard of people who have seen Red Eyes too.–*gayle*

Mystery House Road

When we saw this road sign in Haines City, we knew there had to be a strange story behind the name. Our first guess was that there was a haunted house somewhere along the road or perhaps some other weird dwelling. No such luck. Actually, there is nothing mysterious about Mystery House Road. The name comes from a 1950s tourist attraction that was called the "Mystery House." The attraction was located on the corner where the road intersects with Highway 17. The Mystery House was a fun place with rooms full of gravity-defying illusions and other trickery that made visitors feel taller or shorter.

Sunshine State Ghosts

in *Lafayette County,* there is an old hand pump that does not need a living hand to pump water. In the small West Florida hamlet of Wewahitchka, you can hear the sound of a ghost train cutting through the night—or at least that's the story. There's one thing about looking for ghosts in Florida: It seems every town and place has enough supernatural tales to fill several volumes.

Haints and hauntings rank at the top of paranormal popularity, ahead of Bigfoot and UFOs, perhaps because we mortals need a guarantee that the end is not the end. But do ghosts really exist? If we rule out all the hoaxes and misinterpretations and study a few of the good firsthand accounts, then we must conclude that something weird is going on out there, and it's not easily explained by science.

There are many theories about ghosts—what they are and whether or not they even exist. One popular theory suggests that they are souls that, for whatever reason, are trapped in an unknown space between life and death. Another hypothesis is that ghosts do not exist at all and that witnesses are experiencing nothing more than a playback of past events that have somehow been recorded in the molecules of our surroundings.

Wait a minute! That's just as weird as a poltergeist slinging cups and saucers across the kitchen. Therefore, we suggest keeping a skeptical mind while weeding out the crazies and examining cases of sightings by credible witnesses.

Catalina's Ghost

At number 46 Avenida Menendez, facing St. Augustine's waterfront, there is a restaurant that has changed names several times, from Chart House to Catalina's Garden to Puerta Verde Restaurant. As of this writing, it simply goes by Harry's Bar and Grill. One thing that hasn't changed is the haunting of this old place.

The original building was constructed some time around 1745, when it became the home of Juana and Francisco de Porras and their nine children. One of their younger children, Catalina, is the spirit who is supposedly responsible for the ghostly antics here—or at least some of them.

When the British took over Florida in 1763, the de Porras family moved to Havana, vowing never to return. But in 1783, when the Spanish regained Florida from the British, Catalina, now married, did return to St. Augustine. There she found that the house in which she had spent the first ten years of her life had been used by the British as a storage barn. Catalina and her husband petitioned the governor to return the house to her, and in 1789, she regained ownership of her childhood home. But she was not to enjoy the house for long. She died six years later, and that ended her story. Or did it?

The house was destroyed by a big fire in 1887 that swept through a portion of St. Augustine, but it was rebuilt in 1888 on its original foundation, and looked just as it had when Catalina had lived there. It's hard to say how many people had lived in this house before it became a restaurant, but everyone who has been associated with the place has reported strange occurrences. Customers of the various restaurants have reported feeling a strange presence in the place, which some believe is Catalina. Others say there is a ghost in the building that appears in a wedding dress. Those who have seen this apparition catch only a fleeting glimpse; she appears and quickly vanishes, sometimes walking right through a wall or closed door. While most sightings of the ghostly bride seem concentrated around the ladies' room, she has also been seen on the patio and on the second floor.

Not everyone sees this elusive sprite; some only catch a whiff of her perfume. And indeed, there is a slight drifting aroma in this place that reminds one of cheap perfume. There is an ongoing debate about whether the woman in the bridal attire is Catalina or someone named Bridget, who lived in the house in later years.

But the bridal spirit is not the only ghost here. A mysterious man in a black suit and hat is frequently seen. This specter has been witnessed throughout the building, on all three floors. There is a rumor, with some supporting evidence, that two men died in this building: One perished in the 1887 fire, and the other succumbed to an illness around 1900.

The ghosts at Harry's do not seem to cause any harm and are believed to be friendly. Many customers come in just to see if they can encounter one of the spirits or perhaps get a whiff of that strange perfume. The *Weird Florida* team actually had dinner in the restaurant, and we can honestly say that the lights flickered several times, went out, and came back on—of course, this was in the middle of a thunderstorm.

Someone There?

I have never seen any ghosts in here, but there is a feeling that somebody is like watching you. I mean, sometimes it's like somebody is sitting in an empty chair at the table with you, but you can't see it. I do believe in ghosts but have never seen one.—*Sue H.*

Fleeting Glances

Oh yeah, sure I've seen the woman two different times. I saw her in the mirror when this used to be called the Chart House. It was just a real quick look, maybe only a second, but long enough to tell it was a female with a white veil on her head. Then about a year, maybe two years, ago I got a glimpse of a woman dressed in white rushing across that side of the room. I got a good look that time, and she looked almost transparent. My friend used to work here, and she said that she saw both a man dressed in black and a woman dressed in white several times.—*Cissy H.*

Eyes Wide Open

Nope, never seen anything that I know of, but I've heard about the woman they see in here. I wished I could see a ghost. I never get that lucky, maybe I'm not psychic enough . . . but I'm always keeping my eyes open.—*Megan*

Man in Black

I haven't seen the ghost, but my husband saw the man in black that they talk about. He said the guy was just standing in the corner, wearing those old-fashioned clothes—what do you call those long coats with tails?—a frock coat or whatever. Anyway, this man just disappeared while he was looking at him. At first, he thought it was one of the actors that work at the fort who had come in to eat, but when he disappeared, that convinced Bill that it was a real ghost that he saw.—*Lynne M.*

Shadows of Ashley's Tavern

Ashley's is a popular eatery and pub on U.S. 1 in Rockledge that has a long haunting history. Built in the 1920s, this half-timbered Tudor-style structure looks more like something you'd find in the English countryside than in Florida, which makes it a good backdrop for its ghostly reputation. Although the place has changed hands several times since it was built, the paranormal antics have pretty much remained standard poltergeist stuff, like dishes flying off shelves, lights turning on and off, patrons being pushed by unseen hands—that sort of thing. One night, after closing, a team of paranormal investigators claimed to have observed a chair levitate and move across the room, where it gently settled down on the floor.

What separates Ashley's from other haunted places is the high number of patrons and employees who have witnessed these occurrences. Although strange things have been experienced through the entire building, the main concentration seems to be in the ladies' room, where women have reported "a choking feeling." Others say toilet-paper rolls have mysteriously unraveled from their spools, windows have opened by themselves, latches have unlocked, and faucets have turned on by themselves. Some women say they've seen an apparition in the restroom mirror of a young girl dressed in Roaring Twenties garb. A former waitress says that in two instances, women have come screaming out of the restroom, vowing never to return. They never stopped long enough to explain exactly what they had seen, so we are left to assume it was a ghost.

Over the years, the tavern has been checked out by numerous ghostbusters, with the serious ones using sophisticated instruments, like TriField meters to measure electromagnetic currents, microwave and magnetic sensors, and special infrared thermograph equipment for detecting cold and hot spots. Investigators have indeed detected unexplainable cold spots, swirling smokelike images, and unusu-

Although strange things have been experienced through the entire building, the main concentration seems to be in the ladies' room, where women have reported "a choking feeling."

al energy fields within the building. However, some spook sleuths have complained that they could not document anything, because either their equipment malfunctioned or their batteries mysteriously went dead.

We've heard a number of tales about who haunts Ashley's. One story says that the building is sitting on an Indian burial ground. Others tell of a boy who was killed on the railroad that runs behind the restaurant or of a girl who was killed in an accident out front on the highway. There are no historical records to support any of these claims. However, another story—about a murdered girl—does have some credibility.

According to the story, the girl was Ethel Allen. She was nineteen years old when, in 1920, she was brutally murdered in the restaurant's storeroom and dumped in the Indian River. Ryan Lewis, who produced a short documentary film called *Ashley's Shadow*, researched this story, plowing through microfilms of old newspapers of the day. He found that Ethel Allen had indeed been murdered, but not in the 1920s; it was in 1934. Her decomposing body was found burned, mutilated, and dumped in the Indian River south of Rockledge, near Eau Gallie. The only pieces of evidence were a nylon stocking wrapped around her neck, the initials "B.K." tattooed on her leg, and a ruby ring on her finger.

Authorities were never able to determine where she was killed, so there's nothing that says the scene of the crime was in the tavern. However, further research shows that in 1933, Ashley's was known as Jack's Tavern and that the proprietor was Jack Allen. Perhaps the murdered girl, Ethel Allen, was a relative of this owner. In his quest, Lewis located Ethel's grave—discernible by a small home-made cement marker—in an old cemetery on Merritt Island in the Indian River, almost directly across from the tavern.

Recovery of Mutilated Body Wednesday Near Eau Gallie

MURDERED, BURNED, CAST INTO RIVER

Miss Ethel Allen Left Home Early Sunday For Wauchula

The partly decomposed nude body of a girl, identified as that of Miss Ethel Allen, 19, Cocoa, was discovered on the banks of the Indian river a short distance north Eau Gallie about three 0' clock Wednesday afternoon. Identification was by Mrs. Finney of Cocoa with whom Miss Allen boarded. The victim was murdered, mutilated, burned, and cast into the Indian river. The only evidence recovered was a nylon stocking wrapped around the victim's neck, a ruby ring on her finger, and the initials B.K. tattooed on the back of her leg. Robbery is not suspected as the motive. Mrs. Finney told authorities that Miss Allen had left home early Sunday for Wauchula. It was estimated that Miss Allen's body had been in the water for at least three days. The sheriff stated that the investigation is underway and that no other details are known at this time.

Weird Florida was invited to join an Orlando-based group called "Spook Hunters" in their late-night investigation of Ashley's. The management had graciously allowed the group, led by Owen Sliter, to remain after closing to check the place out. Sliter, who jokingly wore a bright orange ghostbusters-like jumpsuit, described himself as a "skeptic with an open mind." While he believes that the power of suggestion is responsible for most ghost sightings, other members of his spook-hunting organization truly believed that something strange was going on in the tavern. Our hunt bagged no apparitions, but a strange floating orb was captured in a photograph of the dining room. Of course, the orb was offered as evidence of haunting by the believers but was explained away by the skeptics as a photographic flaw.

As for us, we can honestly say that Ashley's has a great seafood platter, but the only spirits we saw were the ones being served at the bar. Yet the strange tales about this place are intriguing and worth keeping an open mind about. We'd like to think that Ethel's spirit is haunting Ashley's, perhaps trying to identify her killer. Who knows?

Experienced the Haunting

I know Ashley's is haunted. I worked there when I was 18 in the kitchen, and things were always jumping off the shelf and breaking. Like plates and cups. One time a knife flew across the kitchen like somebody threw it, but nobody was there but me and the cook. The worst times are after the place closes. I used to clean up and would be there all by myself, and I could hear all kinds of noises, like voices or people walking. I finally quit because I didn't like being there by myself at night.—*J.S.*

Haunted by the Dead Girl

You should check out Ashley's Tavern in Rockledge on U.S. 1. Even the manager believes it's haunted, and I've talked to many workers, and the bartender, and they all say the same thing.—*Sharon H.*

Something IS Going On There!

I can only say that I believe that something is going on there, and it is probably something like poltergeist activity. I think it is some kind of psychic energy being projected by one of the people that work there. I say this because almost everything that has been reported about the place has to do with objects moving or things floating in the air. But something weird is going on there, and it ought to be looked into by scientists. —*Randy*

Ethel Is It, and It Is Ethel

Ethel Allen was killed there in the '20s or '30s, and the activity at Ashley's is most likely the spirit of her. It is a fact that she was murdered and they found her body in the Indian River. It is also a fact that she worked at the tavern. I have read the old newspaper article that is available to anyone at the Brevard County library. I do not think the other stories about Ashley's hold any water; if there is a ghost, then it is Ethel.—*Rubyring*

It's a Damn Poltergeist!

Ashley's sounds like a case of poltergeist activity, which may not be a ghost but energy emitting from a living person. Read some accounts about poltergeist cases, and in almost every one, there will be an adolescent female involved. In my opinion, it's a damn poltergeist! It is strange but true.—*laxride*

It Really Happened to Me!

I have been a customer of Ashley's tavern for years. I can say that on two occasions I did experience something strange. Once when the mirror in the women's bathroom fogged up while I was looking at it. There was no reason for this to happen. In the other time, I had a drink sitting on the bar, and the glass just tipped over by itself. I did not knock it over; it just fell over by itself. It really happened to me.—*coco32*

St. Francis Inn

This is one of the oldest places in St. Augustine, built in 1791 by Gaspar Garcia. Today, it is a beautiful bed-and-breakfast but with a ghost.

In the mid-1800s, the building was acquired by William Hardee, who would later serve as a general in the Confederate army. He eventually sold the building to one John Wilson, who added a third floor to the original two-story dwelling. Behind the building is a small slave cabin, which is used today as guest quarters.

The ghost that haunts the St. Francis Inn is that of an African American girl, who has made her appearances to guests in the hallway and in room 3A. Her hand has also been seen resting on the banister of the stairway. Apparently, this spirit is playful, turning on lights in the middle of the night or changing the temperature of the water while someone is showering. Guests have reported hearing strange moaning sounds that could not be explained.

There is a sad but romantic tale behind the haunting. According to the story, a nephew of General Hardee's was staying at the inn prior to the Civil War and fell in love with a black slave girl. It is believed that the girl's name was Lilly. Interracial relationships were forbidden, so the couple was left to carry on their romance in secret. This was more than the young man could take. Despairing of ever being able to enjoy his love openly, he committed suicide. It is not clear if he killed himself at the inn or some other place.

Lilly carried her grief to her grave, and it is said that this is why she still wanders through the building. Many sightings of her have been on the third floor, which may have been the secret rendezvous spot for the forbidden lovers. If you ever stay at the St. Francis Inn, don't be alarmed if you encounter Lilly. She is a friendly spirit.

The Huguenot Cemetery

There are two ancient cemeteries in St. Augustine within a stone's throw of each other: the Tolomato Catholic Cemetery on Cordova Street, long closed, and the Huguenot Cemetery, just across from the old city gates. The Huguenot Cemetery was also the public burial ground. It was opened in 1821, just in time for the yellow fever epidemic that took its dreadful toll on St. Augustine's citizenry.

The Huguenot Cemetery is the most haunted cemetery in the Ancient City; you might say it is "Spirit Central," because of the number of stories about wispy ghosts seen in the trees, orbs of lights floating among the stones, or a transparent young girl in a white dress who appears sometimes between midnight and 2 A.M. on top of the city gates. According to that story, during the yellow fever epidemic, the body of a 14-year-old girl in a white dress was dumped at the gates. No one ever claimed her, and she was buried in the Huguenot Cemetery.

But the best ghost tale is that of old Judge John B. Stickney. Following the Civil War, he moved from Massachusetts to St. Augustine, where at different times he served as a state's attorney and a district attorney. But to local southerners, he was just another big shot, a politicking carpetbagger who was taking advantage of the Reconstruction period.

In 1882, Judge Stickney made a business trip to Washington, D.C., despite feeling under the weather. The journey was long and exhausting, and by the time the judge reached Washington he was feeling really bad. A doctor was summoned to tend to the judge, but despite the physician's best efforts, within five days the judge was dead as a doornail. The death was blamed on typhoid fever and a brain hemorrhage.

Stickney's body was transported back to St. Augustine, where a big funeral was held at the Trinity Episcopal Church. Every bigwig for miles around came to pay respects. The judge was then carried to the Huguenot Cemetery, where he was laid to rest on November 5, 1882—that is, until 1903, when his children had him dug up for reburial in Washington, D.C. This would be Judge Stickney's second trip as a dead man between Florida and Washington. But that's not the weird part of this story.

George Wells was hired to dig up the judge and prepare his remains for the trip to Washington. A big crowd gathered around to gawk as Wells got the casket out of the ground and flipped open the lid. Everybody was amazed to find that after twenty-one years, the judge was in an excellent state of preservation, though still dead, of course. Then the crowd turned toward a loud noise down the road—it was two drunks singing and carrying on. Before anyone knew what happened, these two men were at the casket messing with the judge's remains. Wells told everybody to move away from the casket and began putting things back in order, but there was something missing: Somebody had stolen the judge's gold teeth! Wells shut the lid of the coffin, and soon the judge was on his way to Washington, minus his teeth.

Nowadays, according to stories, old Judge Stickney can still be seen roaming the grounds of the Huguenot Cemetery, presumably looking for his gold teeth or maybe the men who stole them. If you happen to be around at midnight, we're certain he would appreciate your help.

Henry Flagler

Henry Flagler was the tycoon who built the Florida East Coast Railroad, running from Jacksonville to Key West. Along this line, he also built several elaborate resort hotels. Three of Flagler's hotels—the Alcazar, the Cordova, and the Ponce de Leon—were in St. Augustine. Today, the Alcazar is the Lightner Museum, the Cordova is still a hotel, and the Ponce de Leon is Flagler College (since 1968).

Floridians either loved or hated Flagler, depending on their socioeconomic level. He catered mainly to wealthy northerners, and to most local folk, his ideas and money were an unwanted threat to their way of life.

When Henry Flagler died in Palm Beach in 1913, his body was shipped by train to St. Augustine and laid out in the rotunda of his beloved Ponce de Leon Hotel. But when the pallbearers began to carry the casket from the hotel to the Presbyterian Church for burial, the rotunda's huge doors mysteriously slammed shut, as if blown by the wind. The big doors were reopened, and the procession continued on to the church.

That afternoon, when a janitor was cleaning up in the rotunda he noticed something unusual: There at his feet, he saw the image of Henry Flagler's face in one of the tiny floor tiles. The tile was first noticed on the afternoon of Flagler's funeral, and it is still there today. It is a fun game for visitors to try to find it.

Some said that Henry vowed to never leave his hotel, and it appears that he held to his promise. Students of Flagler College have had many ghostly experiences that are believed to be either Henry or his second wife, Alice. Ask any student about the haunting of Flagler College and most will respond with a ghost story they've heard—or perhaps their own encounter with Henry.

Midnight in the Castillo

The Castillo de San Marcos in St. Augustine is America's only true medieval structure. The Spanish began building the fort in 1672, taking twenty-three back-breaking years to complete it. It is built from coquina, an indigenous composition of bonded shells that can easily absorb the impact of a cannonball. The fort has experienced many attacks, but it has never been conquered.

Through its long history, the Castillo de San Marcos has held untold numbers of prisoners, including Seminole Indians, Geronimo's Chiricahua band, pirates, and prisoners of war. The famous Seminole leader Osceola was held here before being taken to Fort Moultrie, South Carolina, where he died. And that's a weird story of its own.

After Osceola's death in 1838, his head was cut off by Dr. Frederick Weedon, the army doctor who had treated him. Dr. Weedon returned to St. Augustine with the embalmed head and displayed it in his drugstore for many years. There are stories about how he used the head to discipline his children by placing it on their bedposts. After the doctor's death, the Weedon family donated Osceola's head to a New York surgeon, who gave it to the museum at the Medical College of New York City. The head was lost when an 1866 fire destroyed the museum.

Over the years, the fort has collected more than its share of ghost stories, making it a promising place to look for the dead but not quite departed. So by arrangement with the National Park Service, that Orlando group again, the Spook Hunters, was granted permission to conduct an after-hours ghost hunt in the ancient fort. The best time to explore a haunted fort is at night, when the tourists have departed.

The Spook Hunters, by the way, include a wide range of members, from skeptics to believers, who use various "ghost-detecting" devices, like EMF detectors, infrared cameras, digital cameras, video recorders, and even a Ouija board. Chief spook hunter Owen Sliter invited *Weird Florida* to participate with his group in this rare event.

A thunderstorm was raging as we entered the sally port of the Castillo. It was dark and damp inside, and the occasional flashes of lightning reflecting off the musty stone walls made a perfect setting for a ghost hunt. The Spook Hunters used the old guard room as a staging area, before splitting off in different directions to try their individual skills at detecting spooks. Standing inside this dark place, we were momentarily transported back to the time when prisoners had shuffled along inside these walls. Using flashlights, we scanned those walls, looking at years of graffiti etched into the stone, though the EMF detectors indicated no abnormal energy fields.

As we stood there, lightning flashes lit up the courtyard, and the sounds of thunder rolled overhead. The deep rumbling noises could have easily been mistaken for cannon fire. They say that if you put your ear to the walls of the Castillo, you can hear battle sounds. One of our party tried this but got only wet ears.

The first unexplainable occurrence happened in the old prison room when Spook Hunter Karen reported smelling a fragrance she called patchouli. This was interesting, because other people have reported smelling perfume here, a scent that some claim belongs to the ghost of Senora Delores Mari. According to the tale, she was having a love affair with Captain Manuel Abela. When Delores's husband, Colonel Garcia Mari, discovered their shenanigans, he sealed them up alive behind a stone wall in the gunpowder room. Now, if you believe the story, then you'll believe that Senora Delores is the woman who is frequently seen romping about, leaving the lingering scent of her perfume.

In 1833, a cannon fell through the fort's gun deck into a narrow secret room, in which were found human skeletons. It appeared that some unfortunate souls had in truth been sealed up in the fort, although some records say the remains were animal bones.

The most interesting event occurred in the room where Seminole Indians were held during the Second Seminole War. Photographs taken in this dark room showed orbs of light that could not be explained. There were no reflective surfaces in this room, no floating dust particles, and the anomalies were caught on digital camera, ruling out film flaws. Following the unexplainable orbs, one of the Spook Hunters reported getting high readings on his EMF detector. He had followed these readings from the bottom of the stairway up to the terreplein or the gun platform, where the energy seemed to dissipate. Owen tried to re-create this reading by following the same course but could not pick up the energy field. All possible causes were checked out, such as motion detectors and electrical systems, but we found no explanations for the weird EMF readings.

During our visit, no spiritual entities materialized, but the strange orbs and unexplainable EMF reading were enough for the Spook Hunters to declare their hunt a success.

Sanford Fire Department, Organized 1873.

Sixth Annual Banquet
January 1, 1892.

Old Firehouse

Barbara Farrell jokes about having the biggest garage in Sanford; that's because she lives in the city's old firehouse on Palmetto Avenue. Barbara, a realtor and artist, bought the old firehouse shortly after falling in love with it on a visit to Sanford in 1992. The firehouse had not been used for decades and needed considerable restoration before it could be transformed into a residence. None of this mattered to Barbara, because, as she said, "It just felt right." By the time she finished renovating the nineteenth-century building, she had turned the second floor into a beautiful light and airy residence that has won several awards for restoration. The lower level is that big garage.

Barbara had hardly settled into her new home's, when she discovered that she had a houseguest, maybe even two. Or should that be houseghosts? While relaxing with a book in her big brass bed one night, she noticed that little pebbles were dropping from overhead. They weren't falling from the ceiling; in fact, there seemed to be no source for these small rocks. They simply dropped out of thin air, making a pinging sound when hitting the brass bedstead. Then there were the sounds of footsteps, but how could that be? It was a two-story building.

Well, not quite. As Barbara found out through research, her firehouse had three stories until 1928, when the city remodeled the structure and removed the third story.

Although she has never seen an apparition in the old firehouse, Barbara does sense that she is living with a presence from the past, and she thinks it could be a fireman. She is not alone in her feelings; several others have recalled uncanny experiences in the old station. Two former firemen recounted how chairs placed in front of the fireplace at night would later be moved around. One fireman recalled hearing a

rattling sound, "Like a dog running with a chain." One night, while the crew was out on a call, a fireman who had remained behind remembers how the doors started opening and closing on their own.

The firehouse, a stucco-and-brick structure, was built in 1887. For many years, it served a combination of functions—armory, city hall, firehouse, and jail. The top floor served as a courtroom.

The first prospect for a ghost may be a man who was hanged behind the building when it was a part of the city jail. He was Percy Bayless, a twenty-four-year-old black man accused of gunning down a deputy sheriff named Cleveland Jacobs. The hanging took place on March 30, 1923. The newspaper reported that "all adjoining fences and rooftops had their quota of people anxious to witness the hanging."

Does the ghost of Percy Bayless still roam the old building? Barbara thinks that could be a possibility.

There are a number of firemen deaths connected to the firehouse. The first was on August 16, 1888, when a young fireman named Harry Ashton fell through an elevator shaft while fighting a downtown fire. In 1957, a rookie fireman was accidentally killed when he was run over by a fire truck. In 1969, the body of a fireman who had been mysteriously missing for seven months was found stuffed in the closet of his house. His wife was eventually convicted of his murder. Certainly, plenty of candidates for a haunting exist in the old firehouse.

But the strangest event connected to this old place originates with Barbara herself. While in a deep state of meditation, she experienced a vision—not necessarily a dream, but more like an inward visualization—that she was a fourteen-year-old boy from the late 1880s living on a dirt street where a firehouse was being built. She could see horses on the street, and the boy appeared to be taking water to the workers from a fountain located in the middle of an intersection. At some point, she saw the boy being fatally kicked by a horse and watched him die.

It might have been brushed off as a daydream, if not for what happened next. Some time after this, Barbara was at a flea market in another part of the state, rummaging through a stack of antique postcards, when one card grabbed her attention. It was an old nineteenth-century photograph of a round fountain in the middle of an intersection. Around the fountain were a half-dozen boys leaning against the rail. There, in the center of them, was the boy she had seen during her strange meditation.

Then she made a spine-shivering discovery: The photo was of Sanford's Palmetto Avenue and Second Street, a mere half block from the firehouse!

Coincidence or reincarnation—or something else? Whatever it was, Barbara bought the postcard. As for the entity in her firehouse, she says, "I just told him look, I'm living here now, and you're welcome to stay, but we're going to get along." As for firemen, each year Barbara hosts a get-together for Sanford's retired firefighters, and perhaps a few unseen ones too.

The strangest event connected to this old place originates with Barbara herself. While in a deep state of meditation, she experienced a vision—that she was a fourteen-year-old boy from the late 1880s living on a dirt street where a firehouse was being built.

New Smyrna's Old Connor Library

Built in 1901, the old Connor Library is the oldest public building in New Smyrna and a typical example of early Florida architecture. The one-story wooden structure with its wraparound porch was originally built several blocks away, but in 1991 it was moved to the corner of Sams Avenue and Julia Street to be used as the local

historical museum. And that's when weird things began to happen.

During its renovation, workers complained that somebody was messing with their tools at night, even though everything was securely locked up in the building. Each morning, carpenters returned to work to find their tools and building materials rearranged.

During the workday, power tools apparently turned themselves on. Public curiosity was drawn to the mystery when the local newspaper ran a cover story about the ghostly shenanigans. A parapsychologist visited the building and reported detecting cold spots in various areas of the building, which he felt could have a spiritual connection.

The unexplained activity lasted during the renovation phase. For the next decade, the building seemed to behave itself while it served as New Smyrna's historical museum. By 2003, the museum had moved to larger quarters. Once again, the Connor Library was vacant, and the weirdness started again; this time it was unexplained spooky things captured on camera by Jan and Matt Bunker.

Then one night, Jan and Matt decided to make an after-dark visit to the Connor Library to check it out. The couple are members of the local historical society and had heard the ghost stories about the old place. They snapped a few pictures through the windows, and sure enough, strange birdlike images and orbs appeared in the photographs. They made several trips to photograph the old building and each time captured unexplainable anomalies that seemed to be floating or darting about the inside. To rule out physical causes, they examined the cameras and lenses, but could find nothing wrong. They have used three different 35-mm cameras, a digital camera, and a disposable camera; they have even captured moving orbs with a video camera.

Jan says she feels that the old building may be

located atop an Indian burial mound and that is what may be causing all the ghostly happenings. She isn't far off base with her opinion, as the Connor Library is indeed sitting on an old Indian shell mound.

Matt is a bit skeptical about the photo anomalies having anything to do with ghosts; he hypothesizes that they could be related to some other unknown phenomenon, like something interdimensional, or perhaps they are a portal into another dimension. He points to one photograph of the building's dark interior that appears to show an extremely bright light. "We could not see that light with our eyes," he explains. "We didn't see it until the film was developed."

That particular anomaly was captured the same night the couple experienced an unexplainable physical event at the old building. They arrived on the porch at the edge of dark to shoot a few photographs through the front windows. "We were at the front door, and it was rattling," Jan says. "There was no air-conditioning system running, and the overhead fans inside were still. There was just no reason for the doors to be vibrating like that." She went to put her hand on the leverlike handle of the door and it moved, "as if someone moved it up and down, but we could see through the windows that no one was inside." A few minutes later, they aimed their video camera through the window and caught what appears to be two moving orbs of light inside the building. The small circular orbs simply darted about the room and then vanished. "Catching these things on a still camera is one thing," says Matt, "but on a video, and seeing them move, is totally different."

The Bunkers have collected a big album full of weird

photographs, but they admit they do not always capture weird circles and birds on film. The phenomenon seems to occur only at certain historical places and especially during a thunderstorm, which Jan theorizes may be due to the electrically charged atmosphere. Matt explained that 400-speed film tends to capture birdlike images, while orbs and light circles are more likely to show up on 200-speed film.

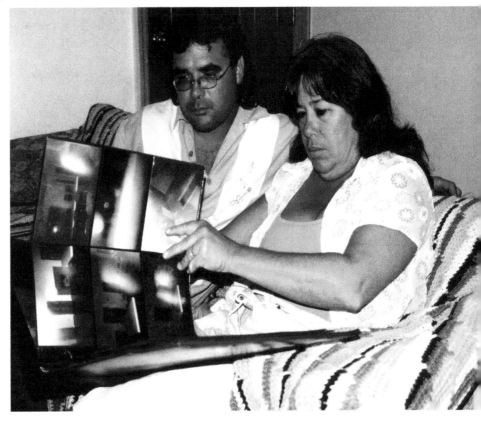

The strange happenings at the old Connor Library have not ceased with the Bunker photographs. In 2004, another organization used the vacant building as an office. From the moment the staff moved in, their computers began misbehaving. Obviously, the Connor Library ghost is still up to its mischievous tricks.

Cemetery Safari

I TOLD YOU I WAS SICK

B. P. ROBERTS

MAY 17, 1929
JUNE 18, 1979

Since the dawn of time, humankind has practiced burial customs. People have tried all kinds of methods for laying the departed to rest, including cremation, mummification, burial at sea, and interment in burial mounds, tombs, and graves. All of these rituals are as much for the living as they are for the dead. It gives us comfort to think we have treated the dearly departed in an appropriate manner.

Whether we call them "boneyards" or "memorial gardens," cemeteries are the only places where you'll find the rich and famous sharing space with the poor and infamous. And if you take the time to visit with the dead, you will soon realize that there is as much humor and history in cemeteries as there is sorrow. But if you go rambling around a cemetery, please be respectful of the "resting residents." As an old medium once told us, "Before you go messing with spirits, just keep in mind that there are more of them than there are of us."

Lynyrd Skynyrd

Southern rock came of age in Jacksonville, Florida, back in 1964, when five teenagers—Ronnie Van Zant, Bob Burns, Allen Collins, Larry Junstrom, and Gary Rossington—got together for a jam session in Burns's carport. They called their group "My Backyard," which eventually grew into the popular southern rock band Lynyrd Skynyrd. The name was a sort of tribute to their high school gym coach, Leonard Skinner, who had constantly given Rossington and Burns a hard time about the length of their hair and had threatened to suspend them.

In 1970, the group recorded their first demo record, in Muscle Shoals, Alabama. It was as a result of this record that their trademark song, "Freebird," was recorded.

The band wasn't an instant hit, however. Its new brand of music didn't immediately excite promoters. But one producer, Al Kooper, had enough foresight to realize that southern rock was about to explode on the music scene, and so he featured the group on his Sounds of the South record label. Since those days, the band has gone through eighteen members and, according to MCA Records, sold over thirty million records.

On October 20, 1977, the airplane flying the group from South Carolina crashed in a swamp near Gillsburg, Mississippi. Killed in the crash were original lead singer Ronnie Van Zant and two later members: guitarist Steve Gaines and vocalist Cassie Gaines. Assistant manager Dean Kilpatrick and the pilots, Walter McCreary and William Gray, also died. The crash was blamed on a miscalculation of fuel and on mechanical problems that caused a rapid increase in fuel consumption. The plane had literally run out of gas.

Ronnie Van Zant and the Gaineses were buried in the Jacksonville Memory Gardens in Orange Park. The site is easily recognizable from a large mausoleum etched with the band's Freebird symbol. In the summer of 2000, someone vandalized the graves, pulling out the casket of Ronnie Van Zant and dumping Steve Gaines's ashes on the ground. As a result, the Freebird musicians were moved to a secret resting place. Today, you can still see the mausoleum and the other markers where fans place flowers, but there is no one buried there. A more lively place for Lynyrd Skynyrd fans is the Freebird Café at Jacksonville Beach.

GAINES

STEVE
SEPT. 14, 1949
OCT. 20, 1977

 ishop Verot's Tomb

Before the Tolomato Cemetery on Cordova Street became St. Augustine's first Catholic burial ground, it was the site of an Indian village. The first burials in this cemetery were those of Indians who had been Christianized by the Spanish. The cemetery closed in 1884, and one of the last to be buried there was Jean Pierre Augustine Mercellin Verot, the first bishop of Florida.

When Bishop Verot died in June 1876, people from all over the state came to offer their condolences. Since the mourners had such long distances to travel, the funeral was put off for a few days, as a result of which the bishop's body had to be preserved longer than usual in the heat of a Florida summer. A hole was dug and lined with sawdust, and then the body was placed inside and covered with ice. But the high temperatures quickly melted the ice.

The only solution was to hold the services early. So the bishop's body was placed in a metal coffin with a glass window on the top, through which people could view the body. Unbeknownst to anyone, there was a problem brewing inside the casket. Efficiently sealed— perhaps too efficiently—it had trapped heat, causing the body's gases to build up. Suddenly the body exploded, blowing out the glass window and spraying everybody with . . . well, let's just say everybody had to evacuate the place because of the horrible stench. The window

was quickly resealed, and the coffin was hurried to a chapel at the back of the cemetery.

This presented another problem, since there was already a priest buried in the small chapel—Father Felix Varela, a Cuban prelate. The stone slab covering Father Varela was slid back, and his remains were gathered up and placed in a pillowcase. After lowering Bishop Verot's coffin into the vault, the pillowcase with Father Varela's remains was put in as well. The two deceased religious leaders rested undisturbed there for the next thirty-five years.

In 1911, a delegation of Cubans came to St. Augustine to exhume the priest's remains for reburial in Cuba. They went to the cemetery and recovered the pillowcase containing Father Varela's bones. They took the remains to Cuba and erected a monument in his honor.

But the story doesn't stop there. In 1975, just a year before the one hundredth anniversary of Bishop Verot's death, Bishop Tanner of the Diocese of St. Augustine wanted to verify that the bones in the casket were really those of Bishop Verot. The only way to be sure was to look for the bishop's wooden teeth and pectoral cross. Workmen used a chisel to break the seal on the coffin. As soon as it was broken, that same horrible stench rushed out of the coffin, as in 1876. Everybody evacuated the chapel until the smell dissipated. A photographer managed to shoot a few pictures of the remains before the lid was resealed. In the photograph could be seen the wooden dentures and the cross. It was the good bishop in the vault. Later he was removed from the chapel and reburied in the center of the cemetery, next to his sculptured bust.

"AND AWAY WE GO"

It's the most impressive tomb in Miami's Our Lady of Mercy Cemetery, but there are not many inscriptions on it. There's only the Great One's name and, on the steps, his famous line "and away we go!" You might expect to see a tomb in the shape of a flying saucer, since Jackie was a big UFO enthusiast. (He had even built a house in New York shaped like a flying saucer.) Back in 1973, he claimed that his friend President Richard Nixon took him to see the preserved remains of space aliens at a secret facility at Homestead Air Force Base. According to the story, the aliens were recovered from a crashed flying saucer back in 1953. After Gleason's death on June 24, 1987, his huge collection of UFO books was given to the University of Miami's library. With his extreme extraterrestrial interests, we might wonder, did Jackie Gleason really want to go to the moon himself, rather than send Alice?

JACKIE GLEASON
1916 - 1987

Phillips' Mausoleum

Calvin C. Phillips of Tallahassee believed in planning ahead, even for his death. In 1900, Phillips built the first mausoleum in the city's Oaklawn Cemetery. The strange tomb was twenty feet tall and topped with a minaret. It was so large that if Phillips had not died, he could have lived in it. After constructing his mausoleum, he hired a carpenter to build a fancy cherrywood coffin and, afterward, had it placed inside the mausoleum. He then crawled inside his coffin and died. In his planning, he had given a key and lock to a friend so the vault could be locked after his death. And that was the end of Calvin Phillips. Or was it? It is known as a haunted crypt, where, some say, you can feel the presence of Calvin's ghost.

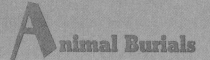nimal Burials

Why shouldn't animals have memorials like humans do? After all, most of us treat our pets like family members. And for some of us, our pet is our best friend. The relationship between animals and their humans is pretty special, as reflected in the following resting places.

The only nonhuman buried in Sanford's Lakeview Cemetery is a horse named Old Bob. Bob, who was big and white, carried most of the humans in this cemetery on their final ride. He had pulled the hearse for T. J. Miller's Funeral Home, and it was said that he could find his way to the cemetery without a driver.

Old Bob spent a total of twenty-eight years pulling hearses, until he was retired to pasture in 1913. He died in 1914 and was buried in Lakeview Cemetery in the shade of an old oak tree. When his original stone marker was vandalized, Gene Hunt, the owner of a monument company, donated a new granite stone. The original marker is now on exhibit at the Sanford Museum. Bob's grave is the most popular in the cemetery. Since his burial, flowers have regularly appeared there, though no one knows who's placing them. In recent years, it has been plastic flowers, but the source still remains a local mystery.

Pet Memorial

This beautiful monument dedicated to someone's beloved pets, Benny and Prince, can be seen in Micanopy in a pet cemetery in a peaceful oak grove next to Highway 441. It is symbolic of the love some people have for their animals.

Brownie the Town Dog

In Daytona's Riverfront Park, there is a small granite tombstone half hidden in the shrubs that marks the eternal resting place of Brownie the Town Dog. In life, Brownie made a lot of friends among the residents of Daytona, so much so that when he passed to the hereafter they buried him in the park with a marker. Some people claim that on certain nights Brownie's ghost can still be seen romping through the park.

Blue Heaven Rooster Graveyard

Down in Key West, at the Blue Heaven Restaurant on Thomas Street, is a rooster cemetery. Resting at peace here are several fighting cocks and even a few cats that had belonged to Ernest Hemingway, who had lived a couple of blocks away. The Blue Heaven, in Key West's Bahamian neighborhood, was once a place where gamblers came to bet on cockfights. Some of Key West's free-roaming chickens are descendants of the old fighting roosters. Over the past hundred years, the Blue Heaven has been a bordello, an ice-cream parlor, a tavern, a dance hall, and a pool hall and was once known for its Friday night boxing matches, which were frequently refereed by Hemingway.

The False Graveyard

This is proof that nothing is sacred to progress and development, not even a cemetery. This little graveyard sits in the woods at the corner of Banana Lake Road and State Road 46A in western Seminole County. The sign reads HISTORIC PAOLA CEMETERY. There are nine old tombstones standing neatly in a row, surrounded by a white picket fence. Some of the markers date back to the 1800s, but if you look carefully, you'll see that the markers are rather close together. The strange truth about this graveyard is that it never existed until the year 2000!

The grave markers are actually from the Paola Church Yard Cemetery, locally known as the Banana Lake Cemetery, which once sat at the southeastern corner of the intersection. Some of the area's oldest graves were in this little cemetery.

In the 1980s, progress reached this area of Central Florida. Land prices went out of sight, and so did the little cemetery. A developer acquired the property, relocated the stone markers, and made a false cemetery. Needless to say, this outraged local folks. The original cemetery had between forty and sixty graves. Most were unmarked. A few had dilapidated wooden markers, and a dozen had stone markers, nine of which were moved to the false cemetery. Whether or not any remains were removed has been left to speculation, but local sources claim that the only bones in the false cemetery are in a mass burial beneath the first headstone. Most of the buried bodies were never moved and now lay beneath prime Florida real estate.

Some of the markers date back to the 1800s, but if you look carefully, you'll see that the markers are rather close together. The strange truth about this graveyard is that it never existed until the year 2000!

Florida's Most Eccentric Burial Ground

The Spanish discovered stacks of Indian skulls on the island of Key West and called the place Cayo Hueso, which means "isle of bones." It's a fitting name when you consider that human bones seem to be scattered all over the place. The first public cemetery in Key West was established in the sand dunes of Whitehead Point. In 1846, a hurricane destroyed this cemetery, washing bodies from the graves and depositing bones in the sands along the beach.

Small graveyards and lone tombstones have been found all around the island, but the one that has become a major tourist attraction is Key West's Old Cemetery. This unusual graveyard was started in 1847 on nineteen acres of land in the heart of town and contains somewhere between sixty thousand and a hundred thousand graves. The exact number cannot be documented because of so many unmarked graves, lost records, and Key West's bizarre burial customs.

The first thing a visitor to Key West's Old Cemetery will notice is the aboveground whitewashed tombs stacked one atop the other, some three or four tiers high. The same stacking has been done underground, where family members are shelved atop each other. The local

name for this space-saving practice is "multiple interments." In one family plot, there are twenty-eight known burials in seven spaces. In other instances, old bones were removed to make way for new remains. In many cases, people buried their deceased loved ones in somebody else's grave. Some families even sold interment rights to their plots, sort of like those time-share deals offered by Florida condominiums. This recycling has resulted in human remains being mixed up with the excess dirt from burials and hauled off to the dump. The problem is compounded by Key West's heat and humidity, which causes rapid deterioration of remains if a grave is disturbed. One concerned sexton, in trying to obtain state oversight of the cemetery, sent photographs to the legislature showing green slime running out of one crypt and down over another tomb!

Even with its problems, the old cemetery represents the eccentric character of Key West, and this is what attracts tourists. All ethnic backgrounds can be found among the burials, and there are Catholic and Jewish sections. One of the cemetery's predominant historical features is the bronze statue of a sailor overlooking the graves of twenty-seven sailors killed during the sinking of the U.S.S. *Maine* in Havana Harbor.

You've heard of Sloppy Joe's Bar, of course. Sloppy

Joe Russell died while fishing with Ernest Hemingway and is now at rest in a boxlike tomb. Not far from Sloppy Joe's tomb is the tomb of General Abraham Lincoln Sawyer, who died in 1939 at age seventy-seven. His final request was to be buried in a full-size tomb. He wasn't really a general; he was actually a former carnival midget who stood only forty inches tall.

On Fourth Avenue, in the graveyard, is the statue of Earl Saunders Johnson; the shoes are really his shoes, encased in plaster. In the rows of graves, there is the one of a black Bahamian named Thomas Romer with the inscription GOOD CITIZEN FOR 65 OF HIS 108 YEARS. One of the most talked about inscriptions in the cemetery is the one that says DEVOTED FAN OF JULIO IGLESIAS. But it's no more weird than the marble tablet for Pearl Roberts, which reads I TOLD YOU I WAS SICK.

Key West's Lost African Cemetery Is Found

It's a piece of America's lost history, one of only two known African cemeteries in the Western Hemisphere. It's not a slave cemetery. It's a burial ground at Florida's southernmost point containing 294 actual African burials, which were lost for 141 years.

The story begins in 1859, when President James Buchanan ordered a naval blockade of Cuba to seize any U.S. flagship carrying slaves. Although slave trading, but not slavery, had been declared illegal in the United States, it was still legal in many Latin American countries. In 1860, three U.S. Navy vessels intercepted three American ships hauling human cargo—a total of 1,437 men, women, and children. Most were from Benin and the Congo region, and all were bound for Cuba to be sold into slavery. It was a lucrative enterprise; human beings could fetch $1,200 each in Cuba, provided, of course, they survived the miserable six-week voyage from Africa.

The U.S. Navy rescued the Africans and brought them to Key West, which was the nearest port. The cramped and unsanitary conditions aboard the slave ships had left many sick and in need of treatment. Key West locals rallied to the cause and quickly constructed a compound of barracks and a makeshift hospital in which to take care of the Africans. Much of the money for the project came out of the personal pocket of the local U.S. marshal, Fernando Moreno. Although he was the main support for the Africans during their stay in Key West, his request for

reimbursement was later denied by the U.S. government. Despite his efforts, 294 Africans died and were buried on a narrow sand ridge along what is now Higgs Beach. Records show that the first one to die was a six-week-old baby, buried in a traditional African ceremony. So many were dying that the government hired a local carpenter to build coffins and do the burying at a cost of $5.50 per corpse.

The surviving Africans stayed in Key West for only three months. In August 1860, the United States loaded them onto ships and sent them back across the ocean to Liberia. Many more died on this voyage, and of those who made it safely back to Africa, few ever got to their original homes again.

Eventually the African graveyard in Key West faded from history. When Fort Taylor was expanded in 1862, during the Civil War, a guard tower was built on the site of the unmarked graves. By the turn of the 20th century, only a few people had even heard of the cemetery. Over the decades, it was forgotten. Occasionally, a beachcomber would find a bone washed out of the sand by a storm, but the only real record of the graves was an 1861 Army Corps of Engineers map that showed nine graves, marked by nine X's, with the words "African Cemetery." It was this map, and the use of radar, that allowed an archaeological survey team to rediscover Key West's African cemetery. Most of the remains now lie beneath the local garden club; however, nine burials were identified, and on March 24, 2001, the state erected a historical marker at the site. After 141 years, Key West has found its lost African cemetery.

Pyramids in St Augustine's National Cemetery

When the United States took possession of Florida as a territory in 1821, a portion of the old St. Francis Barracks' land was set aside for a small post cemetery. The first soldiers buried here were casualties of the Seminole Indian Wars. However, most were first buried at different posts around the territory.

In 1842, the army relocated the remains of 1,400 soldiers from temporary burial sites all over the territory to St. Augustine for reinterment in three mass graves. Three big pyramids were constructed from coquina rock to mark the graves. In 1885, the St. Augustine Post Cemetery was officially designated a national cemetery. A tall obelisk memorial was erected at the site of the pyramids to honor the deceased soldiers and Indian scouts of the Seminole wars. The U.S. government would not provide funds for the memorial, so it was paid for by each soldier in St. Augustine donating one day's pay. At 1.36 acres, St. Augustine's National Cemetery is one of the smallest in the country.

The U.S. government would not provide funds for the memorial, so it was paid for by each soldier in St. Augustine donating one day's pay.

Abandoned and Forgotten

Florida is always changing, constantly tearing down and replacing old places with new. With urban sprawl swallowing up a good portion of the Sunshine State, nothing is safe from the developers' bulldozers. Even old cemeteries have been leveled to make way for new shopping centers and roads. Some places, it is true, have been preserved for their historical value or for their potential to make a buck as a tourist attraction.

On the other hand, scattered across the peninsula there are hundreds of abandoned places that will never be saved though they have interesting histories: The real estate they sit on is just too valuable. These are the run-down structures in overgrown fields, or that weird building beside the road, or the mysterious graffiti-covered concrete ruins that we wonder about as we fly by on the highway at seventy miles per hour.

They are part of what we call Florida's rusting and rotting history. That old building that you see today will be gone tomorrow, and with it will go its story. For some of the places featured in this chapter, this book will be the only historical testament to their existence. See them before they vanish forever.

Cuban Crisis Leftover

In 1962, the Cuban Missile Crisis called for an immediate defense buildup of South Florida. Within a week, the entire tip of the state became an armed fortress, with military units scattered from Miami down through the Keys and across the mosquito-infested Everglades. The main defensive units consisted of a dozen strategically placed Hawk and Nike missile batteries, with their nuclear surface-to-air missiles aimed at Cuba, just ninety miles away.

Did we say nuclear warheads? According to a veteran who was stationed at one of these batteries in 1965, the Nike and Hawk missiles in South Florida did indeed have nuclear payloads, but at the time, this information was classified and thus withheld from the public. Each battery had twelve missiles aimed at Cuba. The missiles were manned by 120 soldiers, who were kept on alert twenty-four hours a day.

At the beginning of the crisis, all missile sites in South Florida were temporary. As time went on, several became permanent facilities, guarded by .50-caliber machine guns and patrolled after dark by sentry dogs. By 1968, there were at least eight air-defense missile batteries in the South Miami area. But by the 1970s, the number of sites was reduced to three, located near Florida City, in the Everglades, and on North Key Largo. About twelve miles southwest of Florida City, a piece of this historical period still remains, but don't plan on visiting it, because it's within the boundaries of the Everglades National Park and requires special permission. However, with the assistance of public-affairs officer Rick Cook, *Weird Florida* was able to explore and photograph this abandoned site in the Everglades.

To get there, we followed ranger John Sears on a twenty-minute drive well off the main tourist path to the site, which is still surrounded by the original chain-link fence. There are three large buildings resembling air

Missile storage hangar

hangars, with superheavy sliding doors. Each building is surrounded by an earthen berm, now overgrown with weeds. These structures were called "magazines," and they housed the missiles. In front of each magazine is what looks like a concrete parking lot. This was the launching area. The missiles were rolled out on tracks onto the launching area in front of each magazine for firing. Each magazine had a firing control room located within the earthen berm, with a ladder leading to an escape hatch on top if something went wrong. (That must have been comforting.) A half mile north, well away from the launching area, were the barracks and mess hall, which are now used by the National Park Service.

Since the high water table in the Everglades does not allow for much underground construction, the missile sites in South Florida differed from many other missile sites, which had underground silos. The Everglades missile site was designated as HM-65 and HM-66 and manned at various times by several different batteries of the 2nd Battalion, 52nd ADA, which was part of the Army Air Defense Command (ARADCOM). The headquarters was at site HM-85, southwest of Miami.

Not far from the three missile magazines and launch pads are a sentry-dog kennel and a missile maintenance-and-

Above: Looking up the ladder to the escape hatch from the bunker.
Left: Entrance to bunker.

control building. The only telltale sign that this place had once been a missile site is the picture of a Nike missile painted on the vine-covered side of the maintenance-and-control building. In the future, this launching area may become a tourist attraction. The National Park Service, at the urging of veterans who had served at these places, is considering a plan to preserve this piece of our history.

Old Citrus Packinghouse

A chapter on abandoned places in Florida would not be complete without including something about the state's citrus history, although most of the old citrus groves have been turned into residential developments and shopping centers. However, one day while driving down U.S. 17 near DeLeon Springs we discovered the rusting remains of an old citrus packinghouse. With a little research, we learned that this place had sat vacant since the early 1950s, when citrus growing began to fade in this part of the state. Yet this area, from DeLand along the Saint Johns River to Palatka, was where Florida's citrus industry got its start in the 1870s. Early orange growers called it Florida's "gold rush"— gold as in the color of oranges. Everybody was catching the "orange fever" and making good money shipping their fruit to the northern states.

Then devastating back-to-back freezes in 1895 and 1896 wiped out the growers. Today, there are not many groves north of Orlando, but a few did hang on, along with their packinghouses. One of those was the Strawn Citrus Packinghouse in DeLeon Springs, the one we had stumbled upon, probably the last complete citrus packinghouse in this area.

The Strawn place is a complex of about ten buildings, where oranges were washed, sorted, and packed for shipment north. When Theodore and Candace Strawn visited DeLand in 1898, they caught the orange fever. The big freeze had left a lot of vacant grove lands, and while other growers had given up, Theodore began buying up the grove lands in 1904 for the purpose of replanting orange trees. By 1913, he had several hundred acres of groves in production. He built a large wooden packinghouse north of DeLeon Springs, next to the Atlantic Coastline Railroad tracks, and went into the citrus-shipping business. As one of the last big growers in this region of Florida, he

Everybody was catching the "orange fever" and making good money shipping their fruit to the northern states.

Today, this part of the state is famous for its nonedible crops—the leather-leaf and asparagus ferns grown for the florist market.

expanded and shipped under his own label, called the "Bob White Brand."

Strawn's success as a grower was not without problems, however. He was faced with insect infestation of his trees, periodic freezes, and overproduction in the citrus market, and in 1921 he suffered a great loss when his packinghouse burned to the ground. He rebuilt the buildings, this time using metal, and it is these buildings, along with a few of the original wooden structures, that can still be seen. From the highway, the Strawn Citrus Packinghouse resembles a ghost town. There is a water tower, some old gas pumps, several small buildings, and the big packinghouse, still stacked with wooden crates. The most modern, and the last structure to be built, is the cinderblock office building.

The old packinghouse looks out of place now, but it stands as a reminder of the days when citrus was king all the way up to Palatka. Today, this part of the state is famous for its nonedible crops—the leather-leaf and asparagus ferns grown for the florist market. Checking around, we learned that the Strawn Citrus Packinghouse, which is not open to the public, has now been listed on the National Register of Historic Places. There is an effort under way to preserve this piece of history.

Osceola Bank Vault

If you drive through the community of Geneva and follow Osceola Road all the way to the end, you'll see a large bank vault sitting at the edge of the woods. This vault, which is actually the size of a small house, is all that remains of the town of Osceola, which had once stood on the banks of the St. Johns River. The whole town was torn down in 1940.

In 1911, the Florida East Coast Railroad Company built a bridge and ran their tracks over the river. With both the railroad and the river, the site was an ideal location for a big sawmill operation. So in 1916, the Tidewater Cypress Company of Cedar Key organized a new company, the Osceola Cypress Company, and built a huge sawmill and a complete town at this location, naming the town Osceola, after a famous Seminole chief.

Osceola covered 350 acres and was a well-designed community, with houses with white picket fences, a doctor's office, a general store with a gas station, a school, a company office building, a post office, and a barbershop. The town had indoor plumbing, a sewer system, a telephone service, and its own electrical power system. After dark, a night watchman served as the town's police force.

The railroad hauled cypress logs to the huge mill from timber operations farther south, around Lake Okeechobee. Each day, two hundred workers at the mill turned out sixty thousand feet of lumber, a record production for any sawmill in Central Florida.

The abandoned bank vault, which once held the company's books and payroll, was the only place in town safe from fire and robbery.

Osceola was a hardworking community, but it had its recreation spots as well. Each week, dances were held in a big house by the river, and there was a "juke joint," where the citizens went for entertainment after work.

"Osceola was a fun place to live," recalls Louise Sullivan of Clewiston, who had lived there as a child from 1934 to 1939. "Besides fishing, we'd pick violets and play hide-and-seek in the stacks of drying lumber. There was an Indian mound near the railroad bridge, where you could find arrowheads.

"The schoolteacher lived with us and shared a room with me. The school went to the sixth grade, all in one room. The water was hauled in for drinking because the local water did not taste good. The lights went out at ten p.m.; they would 'blink' a warning to let us know it was time for bed. Then the electric was shut down until the whistle blew the next morning."

By 1939, the Osceola Cypress Company had started moving its operations to Port Everglades. In 1940, the last residents of the town moved out, and the buildings were dismantled and sold off for lumber. During World War II, the U.S. government purchased a large tract of land in Osceola and built an auxiliary airfield for training navy fighter pilots. In recent times, this area has been used as a Seminole County landfill. The only reminder of the former town is the old abandoned bank vault sitting in the woods at the end of Osceola Road.

Xanadu

In Kissimmee, on U.S. Highway 192, there is a weird abandoned structure that resembles a cluster of giant igloos. These white-domed pods, built in 1983 by architect Roy Mason, were to constitute the Home of the Future, a 6,240-square-foot tourist attraction offering a look at a fully automated home. Called Xanadu, it cost about $300,000 to build and featured automatic plumbing systems, walls of video screens, a computerized kitchen, and various other futuristic features.

In the kitchen, four microcomputers played the role of family dietitian, planning meals according to a person's height, weight, age, and level of activity. An automatic chef moved food from the refrigerator to the microwave to the table. The system kept track of the grocery inventory, and there was a teleshopping system, with its own video catalogue of grocery items that could be purchased and paid for through a link with Xanadu's telebanking system. The house had its own greenhouse, with a computer that monitored the water level, soil content, sunlight, humidity, and ventilation of plants. It also featured the first modern work-at-home office, with electronic mail, ways to manage investments, information systems, bookkeeping, and news services. It even had its own family learning center, with four talking microcomputers and educational software.

Feeling blue? In this house, while lying on your own couch you could talk to a shrink by using a built-in interactive psychoanalysis system. A biofeedback device could regulate background music and project abstract patterns on the walls according to your moods. Hey, with a house like this, why would you ever need to leave it?

The five-inch-thick walls of the structure were constructed by inflating giant balloons and spraying them inside and out with insulation foam. The result was an energy-efficient house, and in recent years, some builders have adopted a similar style of construction.

The Home of the Future featured an intercom system, faucets that turned on automatically when a glass was placed beneath them, a Jacuzzi that used water heated by solar energy, a sensory-deprivation bathtub that gave the bather the equivalent of four hours' sleep in only ten minutes, and closets that cleaned clothes using ultraviolet light and ultrasound.

During the brief time that Xanadu was open, tourists paid $5.95 to tour the fifteen rooms of this weird home. When we visited, the place had long been abandoned but was still in an amazingly good state, although the interior

was littered with debris left behind by transients. (In the past few years, homeless people have been hanging out there.)

Today, Xanadu is just another abandoned place left behind in the dust of progressing technology. But in 1983 it was certainly ahead of its time, and nowadays some of its technology is common in new homes.

Xanadu (the House, Not the Olivia Newton-John Movie)

I remember seeing a documentary about the construction of this place when it was originally built. It was fascinating to see the skeleton simply inflated; then they sprayed this goo all over it, which hardened to create the structure. I was really impressed with it. It's so sad to see something that used to be so impressive go to such a state. But, on the bright side, it's a supercool abandoned place!—*Markus*

Xanadu: Days of Future Past

This is just a craaaaazy place. It was built back in the '80s to be a kinda computer-controlled "house of the future"—like in that Simpsons' episode, and it looked like a mix between Luke Skywalker's house and a white hobbit abode! I actually visited the place. Way back in 1983, I was like 10 years old, and we went to Florida for a family vacation, and one of the things we did there was take a tour of Xanadu. I remember watching the *Thriller* video projected onto some huge screen inside the "Auto Oasis," the computer-controlled party room! The whole house was controlled by computers—in the kitchen, microcomputers could recommend and prepare menus of food chosen according to your specific age, size, activity level, etc. They could also adjust the dining room's lighting and even play music according to the type of meal served! And you could change the view of the outside through the windows to a variety of computer-generated images in case you got bored of the view! Crazy, eh?

Anyway that place made a huge impression on my wee little brain. I wanted to move right in.—*Shady*

The Bat House

In the 1920s, during the big Florida land boom, Richter Clyde Perky came to Sugarloaf Key with the idea of creating a lodge for wealthy tourists. He built a road to connect his property to the main highway and named the place "Perky." But there was one big problem with the plan: mosquitoes—millions of them. Certainly, no wealthy tourist would pay good money to put up with that misery. Mr. Perky knew that he had to do something about the bloodsucking skeeter situation.

He read where bats loved to eat mosquitoes, so he contacted Dr. Charles Campbell of San Antonio, who had spent decades experimenting with bats in an effort to reduce malaria-spreading mosquitoes in Texas. In 1908, Campbell had constructed his first bat-roosting tower, near San Antonio; by 1930, he had built sixteen such towers in the United States and Italy.

Dr. Campbell supplied Perky with plans for building a bat tower on Sugarloaf Key. Fred Johnson of Key West was hired to build the weird structure—a pyramid-shaped bat hotel standing thirty feet high on concrete pillars and having four shingled sides and louvered openings on the front. Inside were roosting shelves for the bats to attach themselves to and a chute for depositing bat guano into a hopper.

For some reason, the tower failed to attract any bats; perhaps it was too scary-looking. Perky contacted Dr. Campbell, who suggested that Perky add some sex-scented female bat guano to attract the bats. Perky did, but the bats still ignored the tower. As a last resort, according to one local story, Perky brought a thousand bats from New Jersey and hired a man by the name of Plutonium Pratt to take care of them. But once released, the bats flew off and never returned. So much for the great bat experiment.

In spite of the mosquitoes, Perky went ahead and opened his lodge in 1939. A year later, he died, and the lodge was closed. Though it burned in 1943, the strange bat house is still standing, even after enduring several hurricanes. Of the sixteen original bat towers designed by Dr. Charles Campbell, only three have survived: the one on Sugarloaf Key and two in Texas.

You can still hear the children's voices.

hostly Children Haunt the Popash School

Popash is the name of a tree that grows in South Florida. It is also the name of a rural community, between Zolfo Springs and Avon Park on Route 64, that was settled about 125 years ago, when this part of Hardee County was still in De Soto County.

In the 1890s, Popash thrived as a small farming town, with its own post office. But when the railroad bypassed the place, Popash began fading away. Most of its history is etched in the stones of the New Hope Cemetery or passed on in the stories told by a few remaining old-timers.

For several generations, the town's old brick school has stood abandoned beside the road. Emblazoned across its entrance is the name POPASH. Strangely, the letters are still bright as new after all these years. Sitting under moss-drenched oaks, the building is an inviting sight for any ghost hunter, and this place is not without its ghost legend.

Some people have claimed that the building was once a hospital and that it is haunted by

children who had died from a fever epidemic; however, there is no evidence that it was ever used for any purpose other than a school. According to another legend, it was built on the site of a wooden school that had burned down, claiming the lives of several children. There is no evidence to support that story either. Of course, the school could still be haunted.

The old building is a disaster inside. The windowpanes are gone, allowing vines to creep into the former classrooms. The school had two large rooms upstairs and two downstairs, with a smaller room that was probably the principal's office. The floor is rotted, and the plaster is crumbling. We warn anyone against venturing inside, as it is quite dangerous. The upstairs is full of moans and groans, especially when the wind blows, and no doubt would present a real scary scenario at night. Previous intruders have left their graffiti where pupils once wrote on chalkboards. A few have scrawled the word "boo" on the walls. We didn't hear or see any ghosts, but the Popash School is certainly a part of local history and, yes, a prime candidate for a haunting.

You Can Still Hear the Children's Voices

There's an old school on 64 outside of Wauchula that is haunted. If you go there at night, you can still hear children playing inside and sometimes a school bell ringing.—*Firestorm*

Strange People Living There

Popash School was closed down about thirty years ago. They say it's haunted by some children who died in a fire when the first wood schoolhouse burned down. The brick school is built on the same property as the old school. I wouldn't go there because sometimes there are strange people living there.—*GT409*

Handprints of Children in the Popash Dust

The Popash School has been abandoned a long time. It is next to a cemetery where they buried the dead. I think the haunted stories are about when it was a hospital during a typhoid fever outbreak, and many kids died there, and now their spirits haunt the building. We went there and saw small handprints in the dust on the windows and window ledges and heard sounds that sounded like children crying.—*tazgirl*

Heard Sounds of Children Playing

The Popash School is not haunted by children that went there to school. It is the children who went to the first school that used to be at the same place. The first school was a one-room school made of wood, and it burned down and killed some kids inside, and their spirits started haunting the new school when it was built. When the new school was closed, their ghosts stayed there. I have been twice at night with friends, and you can hear the sounds of children playing if you are quiet and listen carefully. It is eerie.—*Kim H.*

Monroe Station

Motorists traveling across the Everglades on the Tamiami Trail whiz by the old Monroe Station building every day, but few of them know the history of this place.

The Tamiami Trail is a 273-mile highway running between Tampa and Miami—hence the name Tamiami. The first part of the highway, between Fort Myers and Naples, was surveyed in 1915 and completed in 1918. But in 1921, before the state could hack the route through the Everglades, the project ran out of money. Barron Collier, the owner of ninety percent of the land where Everglades City now stands, made a deal with the state: He would finish the highway if the state would name a county for him. The state, recognizing a good deal, agreed.

On May 8, 1923, Collier County was carved out of Lee County, and Barron Collier assembled laborers and engineers in a camp at Everglades City and went to work, finishing the last eighty miles of highway, which turned out to be the toughest part. Laborers fought mosquitoes and sweltering heat for about $75 to $150 a month. By 1926, Collier had spent $25,000 per mile on the road, but he was determined to finish the task. The Tamiami Trail officially opened for traffic in 1928.

To patrol the new highway, Collier created the Southwest Mounted Police, his own private motorcycle police force. During the bootlegging days, Collier's motorcycle cops chased many rumrunners across the Everglades on the Tamiami Trail. Al Capone was known to have used the highway as a quick route to Miami.

The motorcycle police operated out of stations built at ten-mile intervals along the road. The buildings also served as gas stations, each run by a husband-and-wife team: The husband was a motorcycle cop, and the wife pumped gas for motorists. These stations closed one by one, until all had been torn down except for Monroe Station. For several years, it was used as a hunting camp.

Traffic was reduced on the Tamiami Trail with the opening of the section of Interstate 75 known as Alligator Alley, but Tamiami still remains a major artery in the state—a tribute to one man's tenacity.

When students fell asleep in class, they were sent to the principal's office and were never seen again.

Devil's School

In downtown Jacksonville, jammed right up against Interstate 10, stands an old brown brick school building with more legends than you can stir with a stick. It is the infamous Devil's School, known by Jacksonville's teenagers as "the most haunted place in town." The old building, with tall white columns standing like sentinels, is supposed to be haunted. But if we are to believe the tales, then ghosts were minor players in this evil place.

The hauntings are said to have begun in the 1960s, when a furnace exploded, killing half of the students, a few faculty members, and the janitor. Ever since that tragic day, the ghosts of the victims have haunted the school building. Allegedly, the place became so haunted that teachers refused to work there, and the school had to be shut down for a brief period. A priest was called in to exorcise the demonic spirits so that the school could be reopened.

If that wasn't enough, the school's principal was a cannibal. (We don't know if all these evils took place during one glorious burst of strangeness or were spread out over time.) According to that story, when students fell asleep in class, they were sent to the principal's office and were never seen again. This cannibalistic principal had a closet in his office that had been converted into a meat locker, where the students were gutted

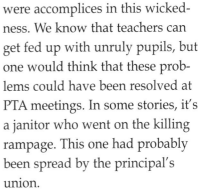

and hung on spikes until he could eat them. Whether or not parents ever complained to the school board about any missing kids is not part of this record.

Then there is the tale about the principal going on a bloody killing spree and wiping out most of the student body. It's curious that no teachers were victims of this vicious rampage; perhaps they escaped, or maybe they were accomplices in this wickedness. We know that teachers can get fed up with unruly pupils, but one would think that these problems could have been resolved at PTA meetings. In some stories, it's a janitor who went on the killing rampage. This one had probably been spread by the principal's union.

The most realistic claim about the school building, which has sat abandoned for many years, is that it was used for devil worship. Attesting to this claim is the satanic graffiti that was once scrawled on the walls.

After a little research, we came up with the real story behind this old school. It was designed by Rutledge Holmes and built in 1917 as the Riverside Park School. It was the first public grammar school in the city and was designated as Public School No. 4. In more recent times, it was called the Annie Lytle Elementary School. It is not certain when it was closed, but the vacant building became a refuge for local homeless people and a place where kids held "initiations" into their clubs. The city officially condemned the place in the 1970s, although transients continued to live there. It was also a favorite place for urban explorers and a hideout for drug addicts.

Like most old abandoned buildings, it presented a creepy backdrop for evil legends. In 1995, there was a fire in the building, which was later blamed on transients. There is nothing to support the claims regarding cannibalistic principals, exploding furnaces, or evil teachers, although some pupils probably thought their teachers were wicked. No doubt the feeling was mutual. The old building is now surrounded by a tall chain-link fence topped with barbed wire, most likely to keep the sinister stuff from escaping. As part of an urban renovation of that area, the building is scheduled to be turned into a condominium complex in the future.

Madness and Murder at the Devil's School

Here in Jacksonville, the old P.S. #4 is supposedly haunted. The janitor, according to local legend, went crazy and killed a bunch of kids. The old school building is also supposed to be the local devil-worshipping spot. I don't know if this is just urban BS, because I have never found anything to confirm or denounce it. —*Anonymous*

Devil's School Is a Spooky Place, Especially at Night

Our ghostbusters club went in there a few years ago and explored the old building. At the time we were there, some bums were living in there. There were a lot of devil symbols spray-painted on the walls, and the inside really stunk bad. It was a very large inner-city school and was used for many years. I know it is supposed to be haunted by the spirits of children who were killed by the principal. They say the principal went crazy and committed mass murder. I don't know if that is true or not. Another story said it was the janitor, so I don't know. It is really a scary-looking place, especially at night. It gave us the creeps when we went inside. —*Kayla W.*

City Tired of Satanic Rituals and Condemned School

I don't know about all the stories other than that there was an outrageous bunch of tales, but there was a kid I heard about that was kidnapped there by some crazed derelicts who were using the place. It became an eyesore for the City of Jax, and the city condemned the building and sold it. —*Owen K.*

Sunland Mental Hospital

This abandoned five-story building on Phillips Road in Tallahassee has long been a hotbed for local legends and ghost stories. First opened in 1952 as the W. T. Edwards Tuberculosis Hospital, it later became Sunland Hospital, a 400-bed facility for mental patients, many of whom were children. Sunland was one of the first places to use electroshock therapy on patients suffering from seizures. There were rumors of lobotomies being performed and of the use of a deep dark pit to confine deranged patients for days at a time. The basement became a focus of tales about a morgue and crematorium that had existed at Sunland when it had been a tuberculosis hospital.

The problem is that there isn't much information available about what really went on there. The stories about lobotomies are most likely fabrications, since there were no known surgical facilities at Sunland. On the other hand, there were also numerous allegations of patient abuse. In 1978, the Association of Retarded Citizens filed a class action suit against the hospital for patient neglect. These complaints in part led to Sunland's being closed down in 1983. Following the shutdown, nine patients mysteriously died after being transferred to a less institutionalized environment in private-care homes.

Another reason the old hospital was shut down may have to do with the fact that it was filled with asbestos, which is a good enough reason to stay away from it. Still, many transients used it for shelter, and so many urban explorers and ghost hunters ventured into the abandoned building that it is now surrounded by a tall security

Sunland was one of the first places to use electroshock therapy on patients suffering from seizures.

fence. The NO TRESPASSING signs are for real, and the police constantly watch the place. Despite this, curiosity seekers still violate the law and sneak into the spooky old hospital, and some find more than they bargained for.

Moans from the Morgue of the Abandoned Hospital

I read the hospital was closed because of experiments that were going on there. All I know is that it is a creepy place, and before they put up the fence, we went inside there, and it is absolutely huge. Even though there is no electricity in the building, the lights will turn themselves on and off for no reason. We couldn't figure that out. It has a basement, where a morgue was at, and down there is where there are moaning sounds. We did not stay there very long—it is just too creepy. I think it is haunted by mental patients who died there. —seminoles04

Ice Cold Air and the Sounds of Children's Laughter

When I was a freshman at college, we sneaked in there—about four of us—to see if the stories were true. We had three flashlights that went dim soon after we were inside, and down one of the long halls, there was a rush of ice-cold air like somebody had opened a freezer door, but there is no freezer there. On the second floor, there was a sound like kids bouncing a ball and laughing. We stopped and were very quiet and could still hear the sounds. We couldn't explain any of the anomalies that we experienced, and did not stick around. No way would I ever go back to that place. It is the most supernatural place that I have ever been.—ghostbuster

Ghost Hunters Become the Hunted at Sunland

There were two of these hospitals; the other one was in Orlando, and it too was shut down at the same time for neglecting and abusing the patients. I don't know much about the inside of this place, but some friends of mine went in there one night. They were members of a ghost-hunting group, and they came running out of there and said that they heard loud screams inside and that they felt strong feelings of anger. They also heard a loud crash, like somebody threw something on the floor like a metal tray or something. They said it was the scariest place they had ever been to. —tallahasseegirl

The Forgotten Gateway to Sunshine

It's a good bet that you've never heard of Boulogne, Florida. It's not listed on most road maps, and we haven't found two people who can agree on how to pronounce the name. Anyway, Boulogne sits on the Florida–Georgia line in Nassau County where three major highways—U.S. Highways 1, 301, and 23—funnel into Florida over a narrow concrete bridge

center. Weary travelers could browse through racks of tourist-attraction brochures and get a free cup of orange juice. If you were bound northward, this was where you could get your last drink of water in Florida.

Boulogne was where tourists got their first glimpse of the Sunshine State, which must have been a bit disappointing, since the "postcard Florida," with palm trees and beach, was farther south. Other than a few palms planted around the station, the landscape at this gateway to sun and fun looked pretty much the same as the landscape in Georgia.

When the Interstate highways were completed, the state closed the welcome center on the old Dixie Highway and built new ones to greet travelers arriving on I-75 and I-95. The only reminders of Florida's first gateway are the ruins of the old welcome center and a big sign at the state line, which simply reads FLORIDA. The old motels that were once filled nightly with travelers are now in ruins or used for other purposes: One is a nursing home, and another is a repair shop.

For adventurous travelers seeking a slower pace, the old Dixie Highway offers an alternative to the Interstates. However, be advised that this old route no longer has a welcome center at the state line, and you can forget about that free orange juice.

Just the same, thanks for visiting weird and wonderful Florida. 🌴

across the St. Marys River. Prior to 1960, long before Interstates 75 and 95 existed, Boulogne was the prime gateway to the Sunshine State—almost all southbound travelers entered Florida through here. It was also the escape route for northbound Floridians trying to get away from tourists.

By 1915, the first main tourist route was opened between Michigan and Miami. This was the Dixie Highway, which used a network of roads marked with red-and-white signs bearing the initials "DH" to keep motorists on the right track. In 1927, the part of Dixie Highway passing through Florida became part of U.S. Highway 1, which runs from Maine to Key West. Since travelers from both the Midwest and the Northeast all passed through Boulogne, it was a great place for a welcome station. In 1951, the state of Florida built one of the nation's first tourist welcome stations here, complete with a large picnic area, restrooms, and information

This page: This abandoned motel was the first encountered by tourists entering Florida, and the original Florida sign still welcomes motorists crossing the state line at the end of the bridge over the St. Marys River. Opposite page, clockwise: The old welcome center; the round information desk that once provided directions for thousands of tourists now sits rotting away; even if this old supply of tourist maps were not water-soaked, the maps would still be out of date. An examination of one showed no Interstate highways in Florida.

INDEX

Page numbers in **bold** refer to photos and illustrations.

ACKNOWLEDGMENTS

One person cannot write a book like this without the help and contributions of many folks. While most of the weirdness in this book is from my personal research, a generous portion comes from regular folks, who have shared their stories through e-mails and letters about some weird experience or place. You know the kinds of stories—the ones that begin with, "Y'all ain't gonna believe this . . . "

For serious historical research, I am always indebted to the Florida State Archives and the many local historical museums around the state for allowing me access to their folklore and historical references.

I extend appreciation to my longtime research associate, Christine Kinlaw-Best, who has an uncanny ability to root out lost history from the most bizarre sources. Special thanks go to my first mate and navigator, Dottie, for keeping me on the right road, most of the time. My thanks and humble apologies to my editors.

And lastly, to the creative directors of this series, Mark Moran and Mark Sceurman, thanks for the opportunity to document another piece of America's weirdness.

Publisher: Barbara J. Morgan
Design Director: Leonard Vigliarolo
Associate Managing Editor: Emily Seese
Editor: Marjorie Palmer
Production: Della R. Mancuso
Mancuso Associates, Inc., North Salem, NY

PICTURE CREDITS

SHOW US YOUR WEIRD!

Do you know of a weird site found somewhere in the United States, or can you tell us about a strange experience you've had? If so, we'd like to hear about it! We believe that every town has at least one great tale to tell, and we're listening. It could be a cursed road, haunted abandoned site, odd local character, or bizarre historic event. In most cases these tales are told only in the towns in which they originated. But why keep them to yourself when you could share them with all of America? So come on and fill us in on all the weirdness that's lurking in your backyard!

You can e-mail us at: Editor@WeirdUS.com,
or write to us at:
Weird U.S., P.O. Box 1346, Bloomfield, NJ 07003.

www.weirdus.com